The Yorkshire Dales

Colin Speakman

Ian Allan Publishing

First published 1993

ISBN 0 7110 2045 0

Photographs © Aerofilms (unless otherwise
credited) 1993

Text © Ian Allan Ltd 1993

Published by Ian Allan Ltd, Shepperton, Surrey; and
printed by Craft Print PTE Ltd, Singapore.

*Gordale Scar in Malhamdale, part of the Mid
Craven Fault*

Title page: Malham Cove

*AA Photo Library: pages 20, 21, 44, 76, 77,
125, 149. Nature Photographers Ltd: pages 20, 76,
77, 148.*

Contents

Other titles in this series:
Dartmoor and Exmoor

Other Aerofilms Guides:

The Cotswold Way

The South Downs Way

The South Devon Coast Path

The Thames Path

Introducing the Dales

THE DALES NUMBER among Britain's best loved areas. Maybe it is the subtle balance between the intimacy of the sheltered dale and the grandeur of the open fellside that so delights visitors, or the villages whose cottages and farms seem to have grown organically from the bedrock itself – the soft greys of limestone walls harmonising with the delicate greens of open pastures.

Yet it is limestone which makes the Dales special. Other National Parks have fine limestone scenery it is true, but nowhere else is it in such abundance – from the great craggy overhangs of Malham Cove or Gordale Scar to the wide expanses of limestone pavement on the shoulders of Ingleborough, or the secret, wooded gorges on the Lune or the Dee where, in spring, rocky shelves are smothered with primroses.

Water is also what the Dales are all about. Not so much in the form of lakes (the only expanses of natural water are Semer Water and Malham Tarn) but in

Above: Langthwaite in Arkengarthdale, the most northerly of Yorkshire's Pennine dales.

Left: Pen-y-ghent.

Above right: Skipton Castle, dating from Norman times and a popular attraction in the town.

Right: The village of Grinton, in Swaledale.

the rivers which flow through the valleys, lending their names to several of the dales – Wharfedale, Ribblesdale, Swaledale, Lonsdale. These fast-flowing mountain rivers, haunt of dipper and heron and distinguished by many spectacular waterfalls, are fed by becks which tumble down the hillsides and, in turn, after rain, are transformed into white columns of water. And underground, water has eroded and carved out that extensive system of caves and potholes which, two centuries ago, earned the Dales the name the Cave District.

But it is human activity as much as natural forces that has shaped the typical Dales landscape. Settlers from Bronze Age times onwards cleared the original forest cover of wildwood which now only remains in tiny pockets. Iron Age field systems can still be traced on upland pastures, while the Anglian ploughing terraces, or lynchets, are a characteristic feature of the landscape. Sheep farming was well established by monastic times, and dairy farming received a boost last century with the opening of railways to London and the Midlands. The railways also brought a growth in tourism to offset the dramatic decline in lead-mining whose spectacular ruins and scars still mark the hillsides above Swaledale and Upper Wharfedale.

Yet the Dales scenery we now enjoy is relatively modern. It was the process of Enclosure, in the late 18th and early 19th centuries, that created the distinctive network of drystone walls amd scattered barns so typical of the Dales. The superb, flower-rich meadows of the higher dales, like the walls and barns themselves, reflect a style of farming and way of life now vulnerable to economic change and the pressure of traffic, industry and large-scale tourism. As one of Britain's National Parks, the Yorkshire Dales are protected, up to point, and it is vital that the conflicting pressures exerted on them continue to be balanced if the area's special qualities are going to survive for future generations to enjoy.

Using the Book

The book is divided into ten chapters, eight of which follow the main dales and two cover The Three Peaks and The Howgills. See pages 8 and 9. The Dales' chapters consist of consecutive spreads like the one shown here.

The vertical photography used in the photo-maps is taken from an average height above sea level. This means that the scale of the photography will alter slightly as the contours of the ground vary. The photo-maps are constructed by piecing together a series of photographs to make each page. They are intended to give a pictorial representation of the ground and strict accuracy of scale throughout cannot be guaranteed. There may also be a mis-match in areas of extreme relief - ie where the land is steepest.

In general, the right-hand edge of the photo-map joins the left-hand edge of the map in the next spread. However, to make the direction of the route absolutely clear, arrows indicate how the maps link together.

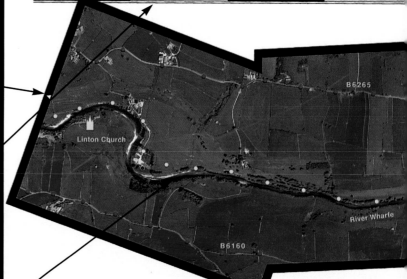

Scale for Photo-maps
The scale-bar represents a distance of 0.310 miles (0.5km).

Vertical Photo-maps
Vertical photographs using a scale of 1:10,000 (0.6 miles:3.9ins, 1km:10cm) have been used to plot roads, footpaths, villages and features of interest.

General Text
Information covering relevant places of interest, history, wildlife, the landscape, and routes both by road and footpath accompanies every photo-map.

Burnsall / Hebden

BURNSALL WAS PROBABLY a Viking settlement, its name being a derivation from the name 'Bjorn Hall'. Tenth-century Anglo-Viking hog-back gravestones and sculpted crosses in the village's medieval church are further evidence of a Norse origin.

Situated by a great twist of the River Wharfe, where a long, narrow stone bridge crosses the broad flood-prone river, and with an extensive riverside village green, Burnsall is one of the loveliest of all Dales villages. It enjoys an almost perfect setting, lying in a sheltered hollow within a great bowl of high fells. The village inn – the Red Lion – is encrusted with roses, and the main street crowded with cottages where mellow stone blends with that of the nearby fells. The present church, almost certainly on the site of a much older one, dates from the 13th century and has two windows of that period, though most of the fabric dates from the 16th century, when it was largely rebuilt. The elaborately carved font is Norman; an unusual feature is the lychgate with a central gate post.

The village primary school is in the old grammar school building. This has typically Jacobean mullioned windows, and was built and endowed in 1602 by Sir William Craven, a Yorkshire Dales 'Dick Whittington' who was born in Appletreewick around 1548. He left his native Dale to seek his fortune in London before becoming Lord Mayor in 1610. Burnsall Feast, held each August, includes a fell race to the summit of Burnsall Fell.

A beautiful riverside footpath (A) leads between the bridge and the Red Lion, passing Loup Scar, an impressive crag overlooking the river, which marks part of line of the South Craven Fault as it crosses the dale. A bridlepath (B) leads up from the riverside to the main road and across to the 'hidden village' of Thorpe-in-the-Hollow. According to legend, because of its situation in a deep cleft of the hills, between the great reef knolls of Kail Hill and Elbolton, the village was safe from Scottish raiders, who didn't realise it existed. Several 18th-century houses and farms give Thorpe an impression of having stood still through time.

Less than a mile along the river from Burnsall there is a little suspension bridge, originally built by a local blacksmith, which crosses the river leading to the lane to Hebden. Hebden is a lead-mining village situated at the bottom of Hebden Gill, a narrow side valley of the Wharfe whose fast-flowing stream, Hebden Beck, drains the nearby moorland. For many centuries Hebden and Grassington Moor provided rich seams of lead ore which, by the end of the 18th century, were worked by deep mines powered by a complex system of water conduits and waterwheels. In Hebden Gill there was a particular engineering marvel: the Duke's Level, a level drain, or adit, dug deep into the hillside to drain the mains. It was planned to become an underground canal, but never operated as such. Stream water powered a number of ore-crushing and smelt mills, whilst the cottages crowded around the beck and the bridge over the old turnpike road housed scores of mining families. Today it is a fine walk along Hebden Gill to the moor and the mines, and it is possible to return over Yarnbury to Grassington.

Riverside and hillside footpaths provide easier ways to Grassington, however. The riverside path is particularly delightful, accompanying a gentle stretch of the river in a shallow valley below limestone terraces lined with mature chesnut trees, which in autumn provide a blaze of colour. Until the mid-19th century Hebden did not have a church of its own and the parishioners'

30

The Yorkshire Dales

Symbols

The following symbols are used on the photo-maps.

Railway station

Place of interest

Pub or hotel

Car park

Church

Youth hostel

Roads

Main footpaths

Secondary or alternative footpaths

Routes referred to in the text

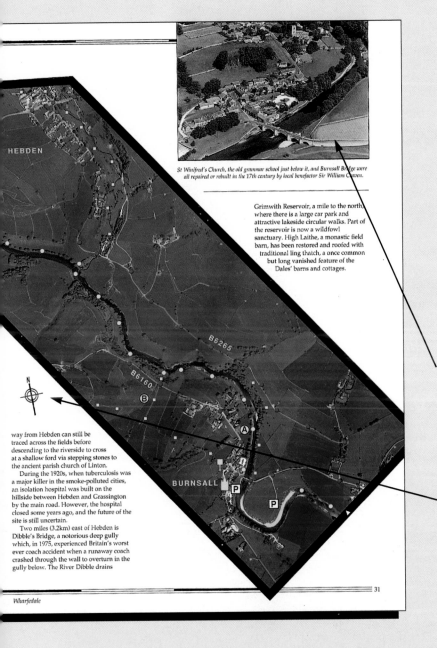

St Winifred's Church, the old grammar school just below it, and Burnsall Bridge were all repaired or rebuilt in the 17th century by local benefactor Sir William Craven.

Grimwith Reservoir, a mile to the north, where there is a large car park and attractive lakeside circular walks. Part of the reservoir is now a wildfowl sanctuary. High Laithe, a monastic field barn, has been restored and roofed with traditional ling thatch, a once common but long vanished feature of the Dales' barns and cottages.

way from Hebden can still be traced across the fields before descending to the riverside to cross at a shallow ford via stepping stones to the ancient parish church of Linton.

During the 1920s, when tuberculosis was a major killer in the smoke-polluted cities, an isolation hospital was built on the hillside between Hebden and Grassington by the main road. However, the hospital closed some years ago, and the future of the site is still uncertain.

Two miles (3.2km) east of Hebden is Dibble's Bridge, a notorious deep gully which, in 1975, experienced Britain's worst ever coach accident when a runaway coach crashed through the wall to overturn in the gully below. The River Dibble drains

Wharfedale

31

Oblique Photographs

These photographs bring a new perspective to the landscape and its buildings. All the subjects chosen fall within the areas covered by the vertical photo-maps, or lie within easy reach of them.

Compass Point

Every photo-map is accompanied by a compass point for ease of orientation.

Key Map

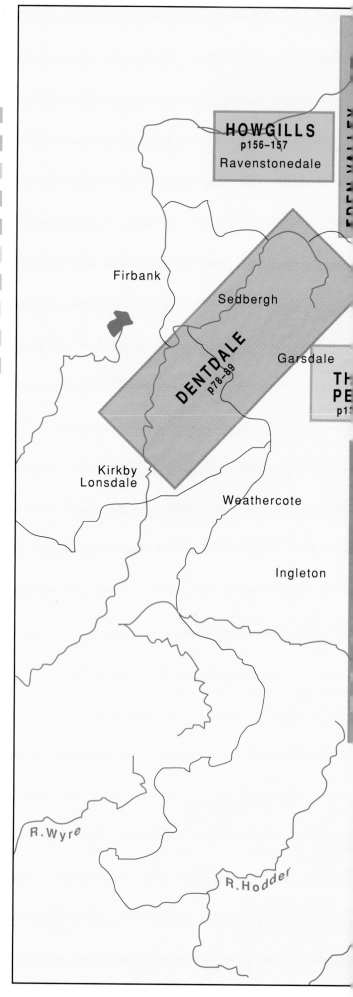

The Yorkshire Dales

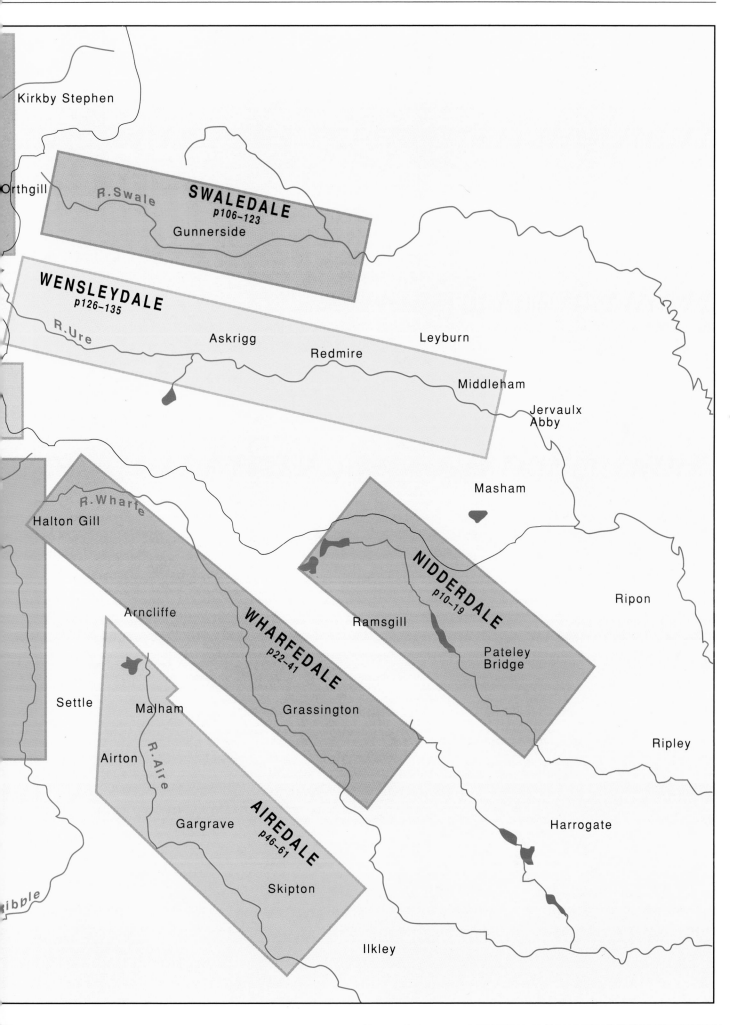

Kirkby Stephen

Orthgill

R.Swale

SWALEDALE
p106–123

Gunnerside

WENSLEYDALE
p126–135

R.Ure

Askrigg

Redmire

Leyburn

Middleham

Jervaulx
Abby

Masham

R.Wharfe

Halton Gill

NIDDERDALE
p10–19

Ripon

Arncliffe

WHARFEDALE
p22–41

Ramsgill

Pateley
Bridge

Settle

Malham

Grassington

Ripley

Airton

R.Aire

AIREDALE
p46–61

Gargrave

Harrogate

Ribble

Skipton

Ilkley

Nidderdale

THE RIVER NIDD runs through the largest and most important of the eastern dales, its river formed from a series of mountain streams high on Great Whernside, along the watershed with Wharfedale, which flow into the Upper Nidderdale reservoirs of Angram, Scar House and Gouthwaite through countryside of austere grandeur and beauty.

It is this chain of major reservoirs that, paradoxically, has kept the upper dale so unspoiled and yet has resulted in its exclusion from the boundaries of the Yorkshire Dales National Park. The need to keep water catchment areas as unpolluted as possible has restricted agricultural and residential development and the building of new roads. But fears of the effect of public access on to the heather moors later led to its exclusion

Right: Yorke's Folly near Pateley Bridge.

Below: Brimham Rocks, east of Pateley Bridge.

Gouthwaite Reservoir with Ramsgill in the foreground.

from the National Park. However, more effective means of water treatment have allowed the Yorkshire Water Company to adopt more liberal attitudes to people walking across their land at the head of the dale, and it is hoped that in the future Upper Nidderdale may share the highest form of landscape protection in the UK by becoming part of the Dales National Park.

In the meantime, a far wider area of Nidderdale, including Pateley Bridge and lower parts of the dale and surrounding moors, has been proposed as part of the Nidderdale Area of Outstanding Natural Beauty. The lower dale has a less dramatic but more fertile landscape, dotted with villages and farms. Much of this area, especially the uplands, enjoyed protection in the past when it lay within the old Forest of Knaresborough. Its game was hunted by Plantagenet kings, including King John, whose castle on a sandstone crag still overlooks the deep rocky gorge of the Nidd at Knaresborough.

NIDDERDALE
PateleyBridge / Wath

PATELEY BRIDGE – whose name means 'badger field' – evolved as a settlement on the River Nidd at the point where a medieval trans-Pennine road from Lancashire via Malhamdale, Grassington and Upper Wharfedale, descended steeply into Nidderdale before branching to the old market towns of Ripon, Kirkby Malzeard and Knaresborough. These roads were rebuilt as turnpikes in the late 18th century.

This mainly stone-built town, with its narrow main street climbing up a steep hillside, was formerly a centre for lead-mining, brewing and linen-weaving. Between Roman times and the end of the 19th century the hillsides to the east were constantly mined for their rich veins of lead, and remains of the industry can still be seen around Foster Beck, the tributary valley of the River Nidd, which leads to the west. Foster Beck Mill, on the main road up the valley near the confluence of the two rivers, has a great 35-ft (11m) high waterwheel, erected in 1904, to drive the machinery of a former spinning mill which produced heavy yarns until 1966. It is now a pub and restaurant. Pateley Bridge enjoyed its greatest period of prosperity as a manufacturing and service centre for Upper Nidderdale in the late 19th century after the railway line was built from Harrogate in 1862. The track bed of the former North Eastern Railway branch, which finally closed for freight in 1964 (passenger services ceased in 1951), can still be seen by the riverside, as can the former Pateley station, now converted for housing. Much of the stone for the building of the town came from the vast Scot Gate Ash gritstone quarries which lie immediately to the north of the town. Stone was carried down from the quarry face by a cable tramway to be loaded on to waggons on the railway.

Pateley Bridge is now a popular tourist centre for visitors to the whole of Nidderdale, with accommodation, shops, cafés, pubs, riverside walks and parks. It also attracts increasing numbers of commuters and retired people, and has expanded in recent years with new areas of housing and caravan sites. The Nidderdale Museum in the old Council Offices (the former workhouse), uphill from the old bus station (open afternoons, daily in summer, weekends only in spring, Sundays only in winter), has exhibitions relating to local agriculture, lead-mining, textiles and social conditions, and there is a restored Victorian schoolroom. The large, circular expanse of grassland immediately by the riverside is Pateley Bridge Showground, which hosts the colourful Nidderdale

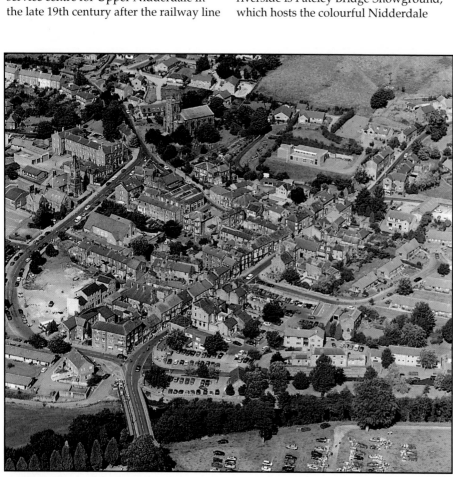

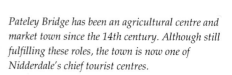

Pateley Bridge has been an agricultural centre and market town since the 14th century. Although still fulfilling these roles, the town is now one of Nidderdale's chief tourist centres.

Agricultural Show every September. At other times it is used as a sports field.

Bewerley village to the south of Pateley was formerly part of a monastic estate, before becoming the site of a country house and park – home of the Yorke family. Attractive estate woodlands and a fishpond survive, which can be reached by footpath from the village centre. The great stone arched pillars known as Yorke's Folly above Guise Cliffe, overlooking Pateley and Bewerley, were erected last century by a member of the Yorke family as a landmark.

Greenhow, 3 miles (4.8km) to the west of Pateley Bridge along the B6265, is a scattered lead-mining village whose surrounding moors and fields are still pock-marked with old mineral workings. Its church, at 1,281ft (336m) above sea level, is reputed to be the highest in the British Isles. Stump Cross Cavern, 10 miles (16km) further west, is a natural cavern system in the limestone discovered by Greenhow lead-miners between 1858 and 1860. The caves have spectacular limestone formations, and major archaeological finds here include the remains of reindeer and wolverine. The cavern now forms part of a system of beautifully lit show caves with a visitor centre, small museum and cafeteria — open daily all year.

About 4 miles (6.4km) east of Pateley Bridge is Brimham Rocks, a ridge of outcropping gritstone crags which have been eroded by wind, rain and frost into a fantastic series of wind-carved sculptures. It is now a National Trust property with good car parking and a visitor centre. There are extensive views from the rocks of the whole of Nidderdale and eastwards across the Plain of York.

Nidderdale

Gouthwaite Reservoir

BETWEEN PATELEY and Gouthwaite the River Nidd runs along a narrow, flat-bottomed valley – a glacial trough – with steep, partially wooded sides carved between high gritstone moorland. Another railway line ran from Pateley Bridge into the top end of the dale: the Nidd Valley Light Railway to Lofthouse, which was originally built by Bradford Corporation as a narrow gauge works line to serve the construction site of the Upper Nidderdale reservoirs between 1904 and 1908. It was converted to standard gauge by 1906 and remained in use as a freight and passenger railway as far as Lofthouse until 1929, and for freight until 1936, carrying materials up to Scar House Reservoir until its works were completed. Carriages on the line, improbable as it might seem, came from London's Metropolitan Railway after the 'Met' was electrified. It is reputed to have been the first municipally owned and operated passenger railway in the country.

Much of the infrastructure of the line, including trackbed, bridges and station buildings, remain, and sections are used as a public footpath, some of it forming part of the 53-mile (85km) Nidderdale Way long distance footpath, including the stretch at the eastern side of Gouthwaite Reservoir.

The hamlet of Wath is set by the riverside below Gouthwaite Reservoir dam. Its name means 'ford', though an old packhorse bridge was built across the Nidd by the monks of nearby Fountains Abbey (they had a grange at what is now Sigsworth Grange Farm). So narrow was this bridge that local farmers used to have to take their carts over by taking one wheel off and pushing the axle along the bridge parapet. Wath Bridge was only widened to take wheeled vehicles in 1890.

Wath once boasted two of the smallest chapels in England, one of which still survives. It also used to have a station on the light railway. The village inn, the Sportsman's Arms, was originally a farmhouse, but was converted to an inn in 1895 to serve the needs of workmen on the reservoir construction works.

Pleasant walks between Pateley Bridge and Wath include the railway and riverside footpath direct from Pateley or a high-level route by lane and path through Scot Gate Quarry. Another possibility is to follow the line of the old railway along the edge of Gouthwaite Reservoir, perhaps returning to Wath via the linking bridlepath through the woods.

Gouthwaite Reservoir was built between 1893 and 1901 to provide the City of Bradford with fresh water supplies. When built, it had a storage capacity of 1,564 million gallons (6,969 litres), contained behind a handsome dressed sandstone dam about 500ft (152m) long and some 80ft (24m) high, with a lodge at the end – Gouthwaite Lodge. The engineer for Bradford Corporation was James Watson and the design was modelled on that used for

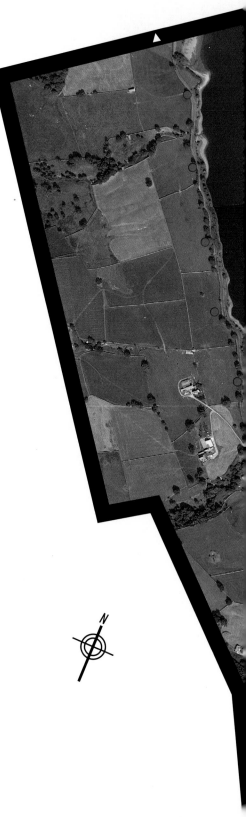

Gouthwaite (left and above right) is one of Nidderdale's three reservoirs, the others being Scar House and Angram. Now well integrated into the landscape, these man-made features have become wildlife havens.

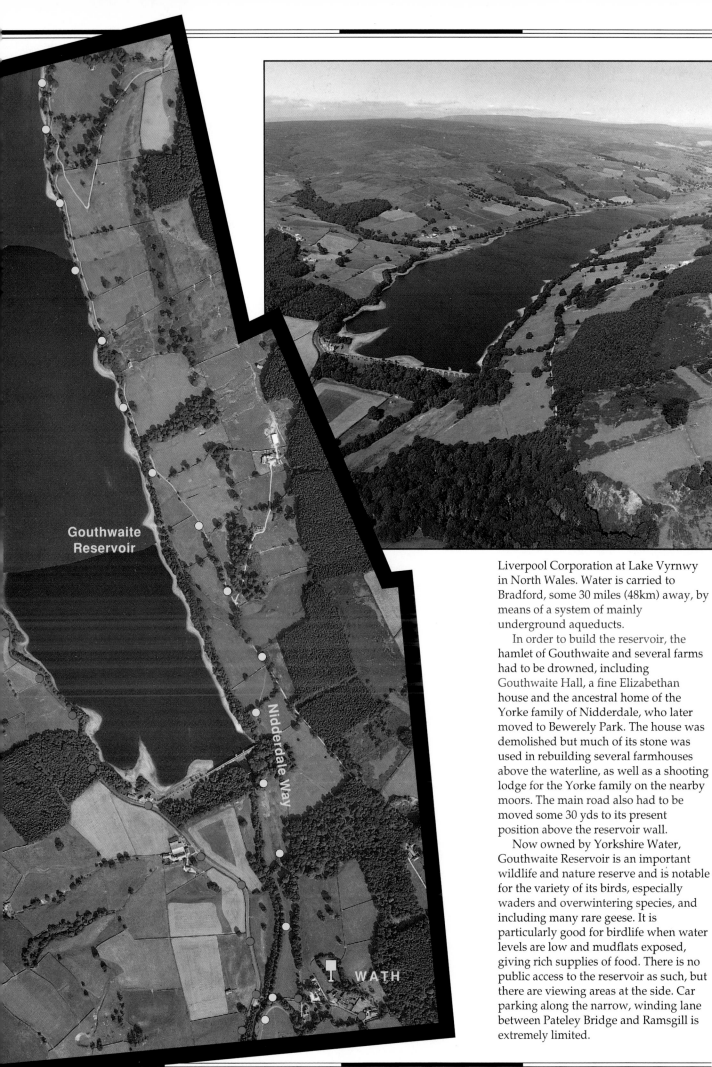

Gouthwaite
Reservoir

Nidderdale Way

WATH

Liverpool Corporation at Lake Vyrnwy
in North Wales. Water is carried to
Bradford, some 30 miles (48km) away, by
means of a system of mainly
underground aqueducts.

In order to build the reservoir, the
hamlet of Gouthwaite and several farms
had to be drowned, including
Gouthwaite Hall, a fine Elizabethan
house and the ancestral home of the
Yorke family of Nidderdale, who later
moved to Bewerely Park. The house was
demolished but much of its stone was
used in rebuilding several farmhouses
above the waterline, as well as a shooting
lodge for the Yorke family on the nearby
moors. The main road also had to be
moved some 30 yds to its present
position above the reservoir wall.

Now owned by Yorkshire Water,
Gouthwaite Reservoir is an important
wildlife and nature reserve and is notable
for the variety of its birds, especially
waders and overwintering species, and
including many rare geese. It is
particularly good for birdlife when water
levels are low and mudflats exposed,
giving rich supplies of food. There is no
public access to the reservoir as such, but
there are viewing areas at the side. Car
parking along the narrow, winding lane
between Pateley Bridge and Ramsgill is
extremely limited.

Nidderdale

Ramsgill / Bouthwaite

MUCH OF THE NORTHERN end of Gouthwaite Reservoir has become silted up and provides a fascinating nature reserve, the River Nidd flowing beween low-lying pasture and marshland into the 2-mile (3km) long artificial lake.

Ramsgill is one of the most attractive villages in Nidderdale. It dates back to the town when a Norman baron, Sir Roger de Mowbray, gave a gift of pastureland for hogs and cattle to the monks of Byland Abbey, on the North York Moors. A grange was established in Ramsgill to administer the estates, with a corn mill and a little chapel to serve the needs of the community. Further grants by the Mowbrays gave the monks extensive areas to the west as far as Middlesmoor and across to the watershed of Great Whernside in the west and the edge of Masham in the east – a total of some 27,000 acres (11,000ha). The monks were given the right to mine, dig, plough and graze the forests, with a 'right of road' for their men, cattle and carts to pass to Kirkby Malzeard where, in medieval times, there was an important regional market and fair for the sale of wool and other produce.

The village has two greens, overlooked by mature trees and the ivy-covered village inn, the Yorke Arms, whose name recalls the influence of this important Nidderdale family. Formerly London merchants, the Yorkes bought this monastic estate from the Crown after the Dissolution of the Monasteries in the 16th century, and established themselves at nearby Gouthwaite Hall to become major local landowners. The inn was rebuilt in 1843.

Ramsgill Church was rebuilt around the same time (1842) in the Early English style, but contains a small gable form the original chapel in the eastern side of the churchyard wall.

The village has an interesting association with Edward II. Until the 17th century there was no crossing at the river at this point; only a shallow ford. In the autumn of 1323 King Edward II came this way with his retinue on a journey from Kirkby Malzeard across the moors to stay at the Abbot's Grange in 'Rammesgill' where he would have been royally entertained before continuing down the valley to Bewerley and Dacre, and on to the Royal Hunting Lodge in Haveragh Park.

Bouthwaite, the hamlet on the far side of the river from Ramsgill, also contained a grange which belonged to the monks of Fountains Abbey. Like the monks of Byland, they were Cistercians, but there was fierce rivalry between the two communities. Fountains Abbey controlled

Ramsgill, at the head of Gouthwaite Reservoir, boasts two village greens, pretty stone cottages, an ivy-clad inn and a handsome church.

The pretty little valley of How Stean Beck lies upstream of Ramsgill (see page 19).

an extensive area of Upper Nidderdale moorland between Nidderdale and Dallowgill, still called Fountains Earth Moor. The monastic road (A), a stony track granted by the Mowbrays to Byland, still leads over the heather moorland from Ramsgill and Bouthwaite to Kirkby Malzeard. There are magnificent views along the dale, particularly along Gouthwaite Reservoir, from this track.

In later years, Bouthwaite was acquired by a family known as Inman, one of whom, known as 'Bold Robin' is reputed to have slain a number of thieves with a dagger which was kept as a family heirloom for many years.

Ramsgill once had a station on the light railway, and though it has long since disappeared, the bridge over the trackbed survives between Ramsgill and Bouthwaite. Attractive walks lead back along Gouthwaite Reservoir to Wath, or a fine circular walk can be planned to and from Lofthouse along the north side of the valley (B), via Longside House and Low Sikes, and returning along an enclosed track part way up the valley side. This links High Brayshaw and Low West House to Lofthouse – a total distance of some 5 miles (8km), with good views throughout.

Lofthouse / Middlesmoor

NIDDERDALE IS A CUL-DE-SAC valley. Beyond Ramsgill the river twists between ever steeper valley sides, eventually forking above Lofthouse into Stean Gorge to the west and northwards along the Upper Nidde Gorge. This curves westwards through a landscape of dramatic beauty to Scar House and Angram Reservoirs, below Little Whernside, where the valley ends in desolate moorland along the watershed drained by the many tributary streams of the Nidd.

The only road for motor vehicles out of the valley is the steep moorland pass eastwards from Lofthouse, climbing over Jordan Moss and Ouster Bank and into Colsterdale towards Masham.

Lofthouse, a compact village with a fountain and an inn, was the site of yet another grange and dairy farm belonging to Fountains Abbey. Its name supposedly originates from the time when an old farmhouse opposite the Crown Inn had an extra storey or loft added. Such 'loft houses' were common in the 17th century, being houses which had boards placed above the tie-beams of their cruck beams to create an upper storey. In fact the name was more likely to have derived from a family name – de Lofthus. The village occupies a sheltered place in

MIDDLESMOOR

Caves

A single, steep lane provides the only vehicular access to Middlesmoor, perched on its hill some 1,000ft (304m) above sea level.

the valley, protected from eastern winds. The old railway station, with its booking hall and part of the platforms, still survives.

Middlesmoor, situated at the edge of the narrow ridge between the Stean and Upper Nidd valleys, is one of the finest hill villages in the whole of the Pennines, commanding magnificent views from the churchyard along the whole of the dale. This agricultural and quarry workers' village was also originally a monastic settlement, this time belonging to Byland Abbey, but before that it was probably a small hunting lodge belonging to the Mowbrays. It had no chapel until 1484 and corpses for burial had to be carried for 10 miles (16km) over the moors to Kirkby Malzeard. The present church dates from 1865-6, though an ancient

preaching cross suggests the site was used for worship for centuries before that. This compact settlement, with its old inn, narrow courts and passageways, is not unlike a Mediterranean hill village, but with grey stone and slates rather than red pantiles.

A steep, winding road and a footpath (A) link Lofthouse and Middlesmoor. A short walk by lane or path from both villages leads to How Stean Gorge, a narrow valley along the little Stean Beck which has carved its way into an exposed area of Carboniferous limestone to create a remarkable natural feature. The gorge, which is served by a good car park and cafeteria, has been made accessible with a series of walkways and bridges. These take visitors under the limestone overhangs to allow viewing of the dramatic waterfalls. Several caves exist nearby, including Tom Taylor's Cave linked by underground passage to Cat Hole, in the car park field, a scramble of some 120yds (110m) of dry cave, a treat for children equipped with torches, which can be hired from the cafeteria.

Just across the bridge from Lofthouse, a private toll road (B) owned by Yorkshire Water (entrance by ticket machine) leads to the top of the dale past Goyden Pot and Manchester Hole, an extensive cave system only suitable for well-equipped potholers.

During dry weather, the River Nidd disappears down this cave system, leaving only an empty riverbed, before re-appearing below Lofthouse. Part of the road follows the old railway line past a tunnel, now disused, through the rock. Above Woodale is a car park and picnic site with toilets. From here it is possible to walk across Scar House Reservoir's massive stone dam. When the reservoir is high and a strong westerly wind blows (a frequent occurrence) water and spray are blown across its top arches, below the walkway, making an impressive display. Paths lead around the reservoir banks as far as Angram Reservoir, returning by the access track on the south side. Walkers can reach Scar House from Lofthouse by following parallel paths along the valley side or along the edge of the moor, the latter giving exceptional views.

An alternative route, for pedestrians only, leads along the ancient track from Middlesmoor across the moors directly to or from Scar House, again with impressive views of moorland summits.

The Evolution of a Landscape

Above: Stumpcross Caverns below Greenhow Hill.

Right: Water tumbling over tufa at Gordale Scar.

THE SPECIAL BEAUTY and astonishing variety of the Yorkshire Dales landscape owes much to the complex evolution of its underlying rock structure. Some 350 million years ago, in Carboniferous times, much of what is now the Yorkshire Dales lay under an immense tropical lagoon. The fossilised skeletons of billions of tiny sea creatures at the bottom of this eventually became a pale, porous rock which in turn was covered with layers of softer shale, with fossilised timber of forests which became coal, then with more layers of limestone and, finally, with thick, coarse sandstones later to be known as millstone grit because of its value in making mill and grinding stones.

Imagine this thick band of limestone being part of a vast many-layered cake, each layer consisting of sands and muds laid down in primeval seas or in the estuaries of great rivers, compressed under enormous pressure over millions of years to produce slates, shales and sandstone.

Slowly but surely the great pressure on the rocks that formed the earth's outer crust caused them to bend and buckle under the strain, lifting huge folds up to create the vast ridges which form the mountains of Scotland, the Lake District and the Pennines. In places, especially to the west and the south of the Dales, subterranean pressure was such that

surfaces cracked along what later became known as fault lines, allowing otherwise concealed rock layers to be forced upwards and exposed above the surrounding land mass, to form the dramatic cliffs and scars to be seen in the Dales today, many of them have been eroded over subsequent millennia by wind, rain and frost into fantastic formations.

Over the last million years or so, there have been no less than three major Ice Ages in the Yorkshire Dales, each produced by climate change and colder winter. Vast sheets of slowly moving ice

came from the north and east, carrying rocks and stones with them which acted like a giant rasp to smooth and shape the landscape, flattening the hills, and carving deep, narrow-sided valleys. The typical flat-topped Dales peak, its summit protected by its hard gritstone cap but its rim weathered into a series of great steps of more quickly weathering shales and more resistant limestones, is a product of both glaciation and constant weathering. The scores of waterfalls that still plunge down the steep valley sides are another typical feature of a heavily glaciated landscape.

Above: Pure Dales country – Swinner Gill descending to Swaledale.

Left: The groups of deep limestone potholes known as the Buttertubs.

As the climate changed the glaciers melted and retreated and they deposited huge quantities of boulder clay and gravel – vast moraines which still dam sections of valleys to create lakes or pools or cause the river to change course. Low circular hills, or drumlins, another typical Dales feature, are mainly formed of glacial waste.

In post glacial times most of the Dales were wooded, with thick forest and swamp in the valleys and more scattered woodlands on the limestone and gritstone uplands. The acid uplands, their woods and vegetation decomposing to form peat, produced surface streams which have, over millennia, seeped into the underlying limestone to create one of the largest and most complex cave and pothole systems in western Europe.

Wharfedale

THE RIVER WHARFE, from its source on the desolate slopes of Cam Fell to its confluence with the Ouse at Cawood, south of York, is arguably one of the most beautiful rivers in England, creating as it does a dale which broadens through largely unspoiled countryside. Little wonder the Romans dedicated a local goddess to the river – Verbeia – noted for her beauty but also her treachery. As this is a river which can rise swiftly after heavy rains in the high fells, and is noted for its powerful currents, this reputation was perhaps deserved, especially before the lovely arched stone bridges were built at strategic points.

The higher parts of the river all lie in the Yorkshire Dales National Park, and contain scenery ranging from the gritstone woodlands and heather moors around Bolton Abbey in the south to the high limestone terraces and steep fell summits in the north.

The riverside footpath which runs along almost the whole of Mid and Upper Wharfedale now forms part of the Dales Way, an 81-mile (130km) long long-distance footpath which starts at the old 17th-century bridge at Ilkley, about 5 miles (8km) south of Bolton Abbey, and leads to Bowness on Windermere, in the Lake District. It takes in the whole of Upper Wharfedale, Dentdale and Upper Lonsdale, passing the Howgill Fells and crossing the south-eastern foothills of the Lake District before reaching Lake Windermere. The Dales Way was one of Britain's first lowland long-distance routes and uses riverside paths for most of its length. It has also proved to be one of the most popular routes, and provides a wonderful way of discovering Upper Wharfedale, even if you tackle it in small stages, either by returning to a parked car via alternative paths, or by taking advantage of parallel bus routes.

Barden Bridge, upsteam of The Strid near Bolton Abbey.

Above: Looking along the dale towards Kettlewell.

Left: The weir at Grassington. A former lead-mining centre, the village is now popular with tourists and a good base for walkers and anglers.

WHARFEDALE

Bolton Abbey / Cavendish Pavilion

IN 1154 A GROUP of Augustinian or 'Black' canons moved from nearby Embsay to new lands in a more sheltered position alongside the River Wharfe, close to the old Saxon village of Bolton. These lands had been given to them by Lady Alicia de Romilly, the Norman mistress of Skipton Castle and here they established their priory. The little community flourished over the next few centuries and despite bad harvests and murderous Scottish raids in the early 14th century, when the surviving brothers had to be sheltered in the castle, the priory became prosperous, eventually taking over vast tracts of land throughout Wharfedale, Airedale and Malhamdale.

After its Dissolution in 1538, the priory and its lands passed into the hands of the Clifford family of Skipton, Dukes of Cumberland, as a sporting estate, and then, by marriage, to the Cavendishes, Dukes of Devonshire. Successive dukes have transformed the

riverside estate into an area of superb woodland and parkland, forming a magnificent setting for the ruins of the priory. Generations of romantic poets and painters – including Wordsworth, Turner, Ruskin and Landseer – and more recently photographers and television cameramen, have been attracted to Bolton with a view to capturing its special magic.

Only the priory church now remains in use, with its west tower, left unfinished at the Dissolution, now roofed to make an impressive entrance to the church which continues to serve the local community. With its ceiling featuring elaborately carved bosses, fine stained glass and handsome early 20th-century floral decoration, this is one of the most beautiful and historic churches in the Dales. Ruins of the priory's cloister, chapter house and dormitory can still be seen, but the gatehouse was rebuilt in the 18th century as a country house for use by aristocratic shooting

Handsome even in ruin, Bolton Abbey, by the banks of the River Wharfe, is surrounded by parkland and woodland threaded with numerous footpaths.

parties, whilst the rectory dates from the 15th century and includes the former school originally endowed by Robert Boyle, of Boyle's Law fame, in 1700.

In the village of Bolton Abbey close by is a fine old tithe barn where parishioners gave their 'tithes' – a tenth of their produce – to provide income for the parish. A large car park now serves the village, which has a post office and tea shop, and the priory grounds. A footpath through the picturesque 'hole in the wall' from the main road opposite the car park leads into the estate grounds.

From the priory ruins you can cross the river either by the stepping stones, the Friars' Steps, or, with less risk of wet feet, by the footbridge leading to terraced woodland paths which were laid out by the Reverend William Carr, Vicar of Bolton Abbey in the early part of last century. Carr was an authority on Dales folklore and dialect. This path now forms part of the Dales Way, which has followed the riverside from Bolton Bridge. From the path through the oak woods there are fine views back across to the priory ruins on its grassy headland above the river.

The Dales Way emerges from Bolton Priory Woods to join the lane and crosses a stream, Pickles Gill, at a footbridge, before following the riverside to the wooden bridge across the river at Cavendish Pavilion. This is a popular walkers' and cyclists café and restaurant, open most of the year for meals, snacks and hot and cold drinks. It also lies at the entrance to the Strid Woods Nature Trail. Car parking is available near by.

A delightful circular walk can be made back to Bolton Abbey village from the Cavendish Pavilion by going out along the Dales Way and returning along the west bank of the river, following a narrow path to reach the elegant Memorial Fountain at the top of the drive. The fountain was erected in 1886 in memory of Lord Frederick Cavendish, diplomat and heir to the Devonshire estates, who was murdered in Phoenix Park, Dublin, by terrorists. A path by the roadside leads from here to the priory church entrance and back to the village.

The Strid / Barden Bridge

THE STRID IS a narrow sandstone ravine that forms the banks of the River Wharfe about 2 miles (3km) north of Bolton Priory where the river forces its way through a gap barely 6ft (2m) wide at its narrowest point.

The name 'Strid' means 'Stride', indicating how for many centuries the gap between the two banks was considered narrow enough to leap or stride across – too often with disasterous consequences. The gorge is, deceptively deep. A tilt on the ledge makes it dangerously slippy and many people have drowned after being sucked underneath the overhanging rocky shelf and held by powerful currents. Perhaps the most famous of such deaths in The Strid occured in the mid-12th century when William de Romilly, son and heir of Alizia de Romilly of Skipton Castle, perished. Out hunting wild boar in the forest, the young man leapt across The Strid but was pulled back at the last moment by his greyhound on a lead, causing him to slip and drown in the raging torrent. The theme was used by Wordsworth in his poem 'The Boy of Egremond'.

Despite its evil reputation, The Strid is a place of haunting, romantic beauty, with the river forcing its way through the narrow gorge in a series of wild rapids. The sandstone banks have been carved and eroded into fantastic shapes by the pressure of the floodwater and pebbles. But the glory of The Strid lies in its magnificent woodlands that now form a nature reserve crossed by a series of well marked trails. Some trails follow specially landscaped paths, laid out in the last century to take advantage of high-level views across the wooded gorge. Many of these paths are rocky and steep in places, but there is also a low-level route suitable for disabled persons and wheelchair users (an electric-powered wheelchair is available) accessible from the car park at Cavendish Pavilion. Alternative access is from the Strid Woods car park on the B6160, but this uses a steep path. Self-guiding leaflets to the trails are available at the entrance to the woods.

Among the many native and exotic tree species to be found in the mixed deciduous and coniferous woodlands are yew, Scots pine, Norway spruce, Japanese larch, oak, beech, sycamore, alder, willow, sweet chesnut and turkey oak. The riverside and woodlands are a rich habitat for birdlife: herons, dippers, woodpeckers, warblers, blue tits, magpies, jays and finches are regularly to

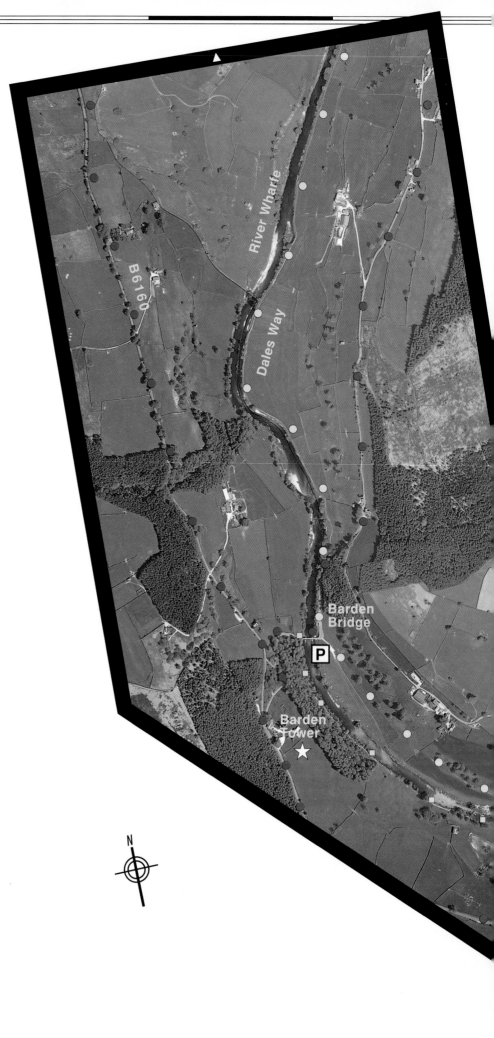

be seen, whilst the woods are also noted for their variety of wildflowers, ferns, lichens and fungi. Rainbow and brown trout swim in the Wharfe.

Footpaths, including the Dales Way, follow both sides of the river past the ornate Nidderdale Aqueduct, which crosses the river at this point. Higher upstream is Barden Bridge, a narrow, hump backed bridge with massive breakwaters which dates from 1659. A short walk uphill from Barden Bridge leads to Barden Tower. Originally a hunting lodge, it was rebuilt as a Tower House in the time of Henry VIII by Lord Henry Clifford (1453-1523). Son of the notorious 'Butcher' Cumberland of the Lancastrian cause in the Wars of the Roses, young Henry was brought up as a humble Cumberland shepherd to keep him from his father's enemies. When restored to his estates after the Battle of Bosworth in 1485, he was illiterate. Much preferring the peace and beauty of Barden to his ancestral castle of Skipton, he was taught by the canons of Bolton Priory and became a scholar and philosopher, and a just and generous

A short way up the valley from Bolton Abbey is the well-known gorge called The Strid. Here the Wharfe rushes through steep-sided, thickly wooded banks, at one point so close together they could be crossed in a 'stride' – hence the name.

Lord of Craven who, at the age of 60, fought bravely alongside his king at the Battle of Flodden Field.

The tower, restored by Lady Anne Clifford in the 17th century, is once again in a ruinous state, though undergoing some restoration. The Priest's House close by is a restaurant, whilst the barn by the tower has been converted to a bunkhouse barn to provide low cost accommodation for walkers. The Dales Way continues upstream from Barden Bridge along the eastern bank of the river through gentle riverside pastures towards Howgill and Burnsall.

queduct

P

The Strid

B6160

Wharfedale

Appletreewick

NORTH OF BARDEN, the River Wharfe
follows a gentler course between open
pastureland, the high moors of Barden
Moor and Barden Fell with their thickly
forested slopes, rising on either side. At
Drebley, stepping stones cross the river
at a shallow point. The Dales Way
follows the riverside path until it meets
the lane at Howgill, the point where
Skyreholme Beck joins the Wharfe.
Tracks through the plantations to the
west lead above the Skyreholme valley
and on to Simon's Seat, a collection of
gritstone crags which, at 1,595ft (485m),
forms one of the highest summits in
Mid Wharfedale and is a popular
viewpoint.

The whole of Barden Moor and
Barden Fell now form the largest Public
Access Area in the Yorkshire Dales
National Park. Access to these extensive
heather and grouse moors is permitted
on foot except for certain days in the late
summer when shooting is taking place,
or during times of drought and high fire-
risk; notices are posted at the entrance to
the moor at such times. A favourite walk
to Simon's Seat is from the Cavendish
Pavilion via the Valley of Desolation (a
glen of ancient oaks and waterfalls which
takes its name from a disastrous flood in

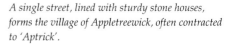

*A single street, lined with sturdy stone houses,
forms the village of Appletreewick, often contracted
to 'Aptrick'.*

Victorian times), returning via the Dales Way and Howgill.

Between Howgill and Appletreewick the river forces its way through another narrow, rocky, thickly wooded gorge, whose white-water rapids are a favourite place for canoers and fishermen.

The ancient village of Appletreewick has a fine setting and exceptionally lovely cottages and houses lining its single street. One of the buildings, Mock Beggars Hall, may once have been part of a monastic grange, though rebuilt in the 17th century. At one time the village hosted an annual autumn fair which was celebrated for its onions. The green track (A) which leads from the north of the village to the riverside is still known as Onion Lane for this reason. Riverside campsites and two inns cater for visitors.

Close by in the Skyreholme valley (where there was once a water-powered paper mill), and easily reached by footpath or road is Parcevall Hall, a Tudor house rebuilt in the early 20th century and now a Church of England retreat whose sheltered, terraced gardens, overlooked by Simon's Seat, are open to the public in the summer months.

In a steep, rocky, limestone valley north of Parcevall Hall is Trollers' Gill, a narrow gorge notable for its rock formations and small caves and the remains of old lead-mine workings. Legend associates this valley with a huge, mysterious 'Barguest' or giant dog, with a single, staring eye in its forehead, which supposedly appears on moonlit nights. Public paths from the end of Trollers' Gill lead across the surrounding moorland, either up to Fancarl Crag towards Stump Cross Cavern or back into Wharfedale via Hartlington with its old mill on Barben Beck to rejoin the Dales Way at Woodhouse Farm.

Geologically, the area around Appletreewick is particularly interesting. Here the Great Scar limestones are exposed, and the landscape is lighter, with sweeter pastures as opposed to the darker gritstone moorlands and more acid grassland to the south. The change is evident in the appearance of miles of drystone walling, built from the stone extracted from small field quarries. In the Appletreewick and Burnsall area, walls have a speckled effect; pure limestone is used higher up the Dale.

Forming a strange barrier between the limestone uplands and the gritstone moors are a number of spectacular reef knolls, of which Kail Hill, north-west of Appletreewick, is an excellent example. Reef knolls are conical grassy hills, sometimes several hundred feet in height, consisting of almost pure limestone. They were created in shallow, tropical lagoons in Carboniferous times from the skeletons and shells of millions of tiny sea creatures, growing not unlike modern coral reefs. A wide variety of fossils is to be seen in walls and in boulders on the limestone.

APPLETREEWICK

(A)

Dales Way

Wharfedale

Linton Church

B6265

River Wharfe

B6160

Burnsall / Hebden

BURNSALL WAS PROBABLY a Viking settlement, its name being a derivation from the name 'Bjorn Hall'. Tenth-century Anglo-Viking hog-back gravestones and sculpted crosses in the village's medieval church are further evidence of a Norse origin.

Situated by a great twist of the River Wharfe, where a long, narrow stone bridge crosses the broad flood-prone river, and with an extensive riverside village green, Burnsall is one of the loveliest of all Dales villages. It enjoys an almost perfect setting, lying in a sheltered hollow within a great bowl of high fells. The village inn – the Red Lion – is encrusted with roses, and the main street crowded with cottages whose mellow stone blends with that of the nearby fells. The present church, almost certainly on the site of a much older one, dates from the 13th century and has two windows of that period, though most of the fabric dates from the 16th century, when it was largely rebuilt. The elaborately carved font is Norman; an unusual feature is the lychgate with a central gate post.

The village primary school is in the old grammar school building. This has typically Jacobean mullioned windows,

and was built
and endowed in 1602
by Sir William Craven, a
Yorkshire Dales 'Dick Whittington' who was born in Appletreewick around 1548. He left his native Dale to seek his fortune in London before becoming Lord Mayor in 1610. Burnsall Feast, held each August, includes a fell race to the summit of Burnsall Fell.

A beautiful riverside footpath (A) leads between the bridge and the Red Lion, passing Loup Scar, an impressive crag overlooking the river, which marks part of line of the South Craven Fault as it crosses the dale. A bridlepath (B) leads up from the riverside to the main road and across to the 'hidden village' of Thorpe-in-the-Hollow. According to legend, because of its situation in a deep cleft of the hills, between the great reef knolls of Kail Hill and Elbolton, the village was safe from Scottish raiders, who didn't realise it existed. Several 18th-century houses and farms give Thorpe an impression of having stood still through time.

Less than a mile along the river from Burnsall there is a little suspension bridge, originally built by a local blacksmith, which crosses the river leading to the lane to Hebden. Hebden is a lead-mining village situated at the

bottom of Hebden Gill, a narrow side valley of the Wharfe whose fast-flowing stream, Hebden Beck, drains the nearby moorland. For many centuries Hebden and Grassington Moor provided rich seams of lead ore which, by the end of the 18th century, were worked by deep mines powered by a complex system of water conduits and waterwheels. In Hebden Gill there was a particular engineering marvel: the Duke's Level, a level drain, or adit, dug deep into the hillside to drain the mains. It was planned to become an underground canal, but never operated as such. Stream water powered a number of ore-crushing and smelt mills, whilst the cottages crowded around the beck and the bridge over the old turnpike road housed scores of mining families. Today it is a fine walk along Hebden Gill to the moor and the mines, and it is possible to return over Yarnbury to Grassington.

Riverside and hillside footpaths provide easier ways to Grassington, however. The riverside path is particularly delightful, accompanying a gentle stretch of the river in a shallow valley below limestone terraces lined with mature chesnut trees, which in autumn provide a blaze of colour. Until the mid-19th century Hebden did not have a church of its own and the parishioners'

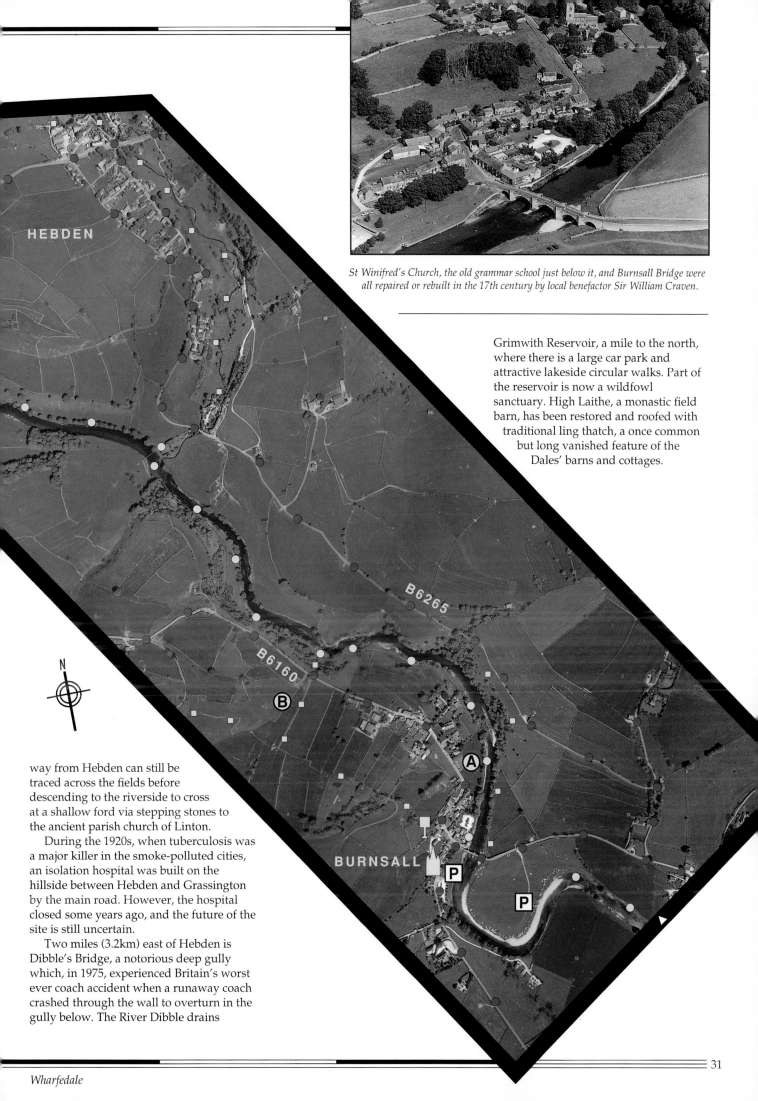

HEBDEN

BURNSALL

B6265

B6160

Ⓑ

Ⓐ

N

St Winifred's Church, the old grammar school just below it, and Burnsall Bridge were all repaired or rebuilt in the 17th century by local benefactor Sir William Craven.

Grimwith Reservoir, a mile to the north, where there is a large car park and attractive lakeside circular walks. Part of the reservoir is now a wildfowl sanctuary. High Laithe, a monastic field barn, has been restored and roofed with traditional ling thatch, a once common but long vanished feature of the Dales' barns and cottages.

way from Hebden can still be traced across the fields before descending to the riverside to cross at a shallow ford via stepping stones to the ancient parish church of Linton.

During the 1920s, when tuberculosis was a major killer in the smoke-polluted cities, an isolation hospital was built on the hillside between Hebden and Grassington by the main road. However, the hospital closed some years ago, and the future of the site is still uncertain.

Two miles (3.2km) east of Hebden is Dibble's Bridge, a notorious deep gully which, in 1975, experienced Britain's worst ever coach accident when a runaway coach crashed through the wall to overturn in the gully below. The River Dibble drains

Linton village

Grassington

LINTON CHURCH is often described as the Cathedral of the Dales. It is situated on a low bank of land by the riverside, some distance away from the four civil parishes it once served – Grassington, Linton, Threshfield and Hebden. The reason for its isolation from the villages is almost certainly that it occupies an Anglo Saxon pagan site and Saxons, believing in ghosts, preferred their consecrated ground well away from their homesteads. The long, low church has no tower – only a modest belfry – and dates from the 12th century. Although it has been modified over the centuries, it has kept much of the simplicity of a Norman church without any of the ostentation of later ages.

Close by, Linton Falls provide a spectacular series of cascades on the River Wharfe. This is another part of the Craven Fault – the line of the Mid Craven Fault – as its crosses the Dale, exposing hard limestone which has eroded into fantastic shapes.

Such was the power of the river and its adjacent streams that for centuries it was harnessed for power. Linton Mill, situated by the falls, and dating from medieval times, was a water-driven wool and cotton mill, which was later steam powered. In the 1980s, it was demolished to make way for housing. A weir across the river provided a head of water for the turbines which provided electric power for Linton and Grassington during the first half of this century. A footbridge – a splendid place to view the falls – links the former mill cottages with Grassington.

Linton, about a mile from the Falls by lane or fieldpath, is an Outstanding Conservation Area. The compact village surrounds a large green where there are a number of unspoiled 17th- and 18th-century houses and cottages, a white-walled village inn, and the Fountaines Hospital – a remarkable baroque almshouse which still provides homes for local elderly people. It was reputedly built to the designs of Sir John Vanbrugh, architect of Castle Howard.

Grassington is the unofficial capital of Upper Wharfedale. Although its origins go back to Romano-British times, it probably moved to its present site when Anglian settlers occupied the area. Grassington Old Hall almost certainly stands on the site of the Headman's Hall, which became the Norman manor house of the De Plumptons. Part of the present house is, medieval. Dating from the 13th century, it has an unusual rose window and is the oldest occupied house in the Dales.

Present-day Grassington evolved around a cobbled market place (the market and fair ceased last century) as a typical upper Dales farming community, but from the 17th century onwards it became an important mining village with clusters of tiny cottages crammed into narrow courts or 'folds' along what were originally cottage gardens or crofts. In earlier times miners worked as 'free' miners, bidding for sections of moor to work for the lucrative galena or lead ore. By the early 19th century the mechanisation of the moorland mines produced boom conditions, but there was also hardship and poverty which was only relieved by the building of new chapels and a Mechanics Institute – now the Devonshire Institute and town hall. The collapse of lead-mining owing to cheap foreign imports and dwindling seams of ore caused Grassington to lose two thirds of its

population between the 1880s and 1900. The situation was only relieved by the coming of the Yorkshire Dales Railway in 1901, which ran between Skipton and Threshfield and helped to make Grassington the principal tourist village of Upper Wharfedale, a position which it has continued to hold long after the railway's closure. There are ample accommodation and refreshment facilities and shops, and the fascinating Upper Wharfedale Folk Museum stands in the Square. The Yorkshire Dales National Park Visitor Centre and administrative offices, by the main car park are in the house and grounds once occupied by the Duke of Devonshire's mining agent.

Grassington is an exceptionally good centre for walking. There are fine riverside walks back to Burnsall and upriver(A) past Ghaistrill's Strid – a

series of white water rapids and cataracts – to Grass Woods (a nature reserve famous for its wildflowers). The Dales Way crosses high limestone terraces past Lea Green, the site of extensive Iron Age settlements, and continues towards Conistone and Kettlewell. Industrial archaeologists can take the cul-de-sac road to Yarnbury, on the edge of Grassington Moor, where a National Park interpretive trail leads through some of the most impressive of the lead-mine remains. Things to be seen include Tudor bell pits along the lines of former veins of ore, old levels, crushing floors, buddles (storage chambers), a powder house, complex water courses, and the huge Cupola Smelt Mill at the top of Hebden Gill, with its remarkable flue system and a tall chimney – a striking local landmark.

Conistone / Kilnsey

THE TINY VILLAGE of Conistone, little more than a hamlet, with its tall Maypole standing at a quiet crossroads, lies on the back road between Grassington and Kettlewell. Some scholars have suggested that the Roman road from Ilkley to Bainbridge probably ran along this route. Conistone was probably an Anglian farming settlement which grew up close to a ford across the river where, in medieval times, a bridge was built. The village is mentioned in the Domesday Book as 'Cunestune'. Its little church, though heavily restored, dates from Norman times. Until 1876 it was only a chapel-of-ease to Burnsall Church. There are several fine old farmhouses in the village, most dating form the 17th and 18th centuries. The village is now a centre for pony trekking.

A footpath(A) from the centre of the village leads into Gurling Trough, a narrow, dry limestone gorge, from which the only exit is a fairly gentle scramble up Conistone Dibb on to the high-level path carrying the Dales Way across Conistone Pastures by High Castle Scar and Conistone Pie – a spectacular line of limestone crags and scars. Close by this point are a number of Iron Age field enclosures and even hut circles. About a

Kilnsey Crag, rising up 170ft (51.6m) above the B6160. Every summer, runners race to the summit.

century ago an excavated tumulus revealed the remains of a Celtic man buried along with a bone-handled knife. A stony track, Scot Gate, climbs over the Conistone Moor to old mine workings beyond Mossdale. From there the old Monastic Way between Kilnsey and Bouthwaite in Nidderdale (probably continuing to Fountains Abbey) can still be followed over bleak and desolate moors before eventually emerging at How Stean above Lofthouse (see page 19).

Another fine but less strenuous walk (B) from Conistone leads back to Grassington, following the footpath across Old Pasture, south of the village and climbing around the Dib Scar and the edge of Bastow Wood past some impressive karst limestone formations, where tilted beds of the rock are clearly exposed. The higher pastures are brilliant with wildflowers in late spring, including rock roses, mountain pansies and the beautiful bird's eye primrose. Common orchids, primroses, bluebells and lilies of the valley are to be seen in the woods – all of which are now protected by the law from picking. A particular feature is a number of concrete dew ponds built to retain dew and rainwater for grazing animals on the otherwise porous land; some of these sites are believed to have

The Dales Way – with an example of the drystone walling that is so typical of Yorkshire – a mile or so north-east of Conistone.

Kilnsey Crag

C

KILNSEY

CONISTONE

A

B

River Wharfe

B6160

their origin in Iron Age times.

On the other side of the river from Conistone is the hamlet of Kilnsey. Here lay the principal grange in Wharfedale belonging to Fountains Abbey. It was situated at the foot of Mastiles Lane (C), the beautiful green drove road which sweeps across the fellsides from Malhamdale. A tiny outbuilding in front of Kilnsey Old Hall, now used for farm storage, is a surviving fragment of the monastic gatehouse of the Grange. Kilnsey Old Hall, a former yeoman farmer's house, was built by Christopher Wade in 1648; his son, Cuthbert, was a Captain of Charles I's Royalist Guards during the Civil War.

The hamlet has a popular inn, the Tennants Arms, named after a local landowning family of the last century. Close by is Kilnsey Park, a trout farm with a small visitor interpretive centre, an aquarium of Dales' river fish and water creatures and trout feeding facilities. Angling is offered from some of the pools, whilst fresh trout are usually available for sale to those with no wish to catch their own.

Immediately behind the village is Cool Scar Quarry, a limestone quarry whose vast cliff face, cut into the hillside in a series of terraces, is visible to walkers from the nearby hillsides, albeit largely hidden from the main road.

To the north of the hamlet, overlooking the main road up the dale, is Kilnsey Crag, a huge bluff of Great Scar limestone which has been undercut by the actions of the ancient Wharfedale glacier, leaving a great underhang which is a challenge to rock-climbers, and a prominent local landmark.

In the fields opposite the Crag, Kilnsey Show takes place each year on the Tuesday after August Bank Holiday Monday. It is one of the largest of the many Dales agricultural shows and has a great variety of prize sheep and cattle on show, a drystone walling competition, sheep, dog and show-jumping trials. Marquees hold displays of farmhouse produce, and Dales crafts as well as other goods are for sale. A highlight of the afternoon is the Annual Fell Race to and from the summit of Kilnsey Crag which attracts runners from all over the North of England.

Arncliffe (right) is the largest of four communities in Littondale (below). Limestone scars edge the sides of the flat-bottomed valley that has provided rich arable and pasture land for centuries.

Amerdale Dub / Scargill

THE RIVER SKIRFARE joins the Wharfe at Amerdale Dub, the name Dub being derived from the Celtic word meaning pool, or pond, whilst Amerdale is the old name for Littondale. This was, incidentally, the origin of the name 'Emmerdale' in the television series *Emmerdale Farm*, now filmed near Bradford to prevent Littondale being overrun with curious, souvenir seeking viewers.

The two Dales are divided by a narrow ridge of high fell rising up to over 1,973ft (600m) and known as Old Cote Moor . Old Cote is actually the name of a Jacobean farmhouse in Litton, 'Cote' being the Old English name for a house or farm.

The limestone crag where Old Cote Moor terminates, overlooking the junction between the two valleys, is known as Knipe Scar, which in turn overlooks a grassy slope known as High Wind Bank. This is a popular place for hang-gliders and on busy summer days much of the area is filled with parked cars.

Littondale is the principal tributary valley of Upper Wharfedale. It is a quieter, narrower valley than its parent dale and has two principal villages: Arncliffe and Litton. Arncliffe has an impressive example of a defensive-style green, a pattern established in the 14th century after the Battle of Bannockburn in 1314, when Scottish raids against an ill-defended England were so common that Dales people had to turn to their own resources to safeguard life and property, herding cattle into the central green, like a stockade, against the bands of marauding Scots. The village church has a sturdy, castellated tower, which, though rebuilt in Tudor times, seems eminently capable of resisting any such attack. Ancient woodlands clothing the valley sides between high fells make Littondale a particularly lovely valley, described with remarkable accuracy as 'Vendale' in Charles Kingsley's Victorian polemic novel of industrial and rural England, *The Water Babies*.

From Arncliffe the narrow, twisting road over Darnbrook to Malhamdale opposite Yew Coggar Scar, a series of exposed limestone scars along the steep hillside, is one of the most spectacular in the Yorkshire Dales. The main road up the valley continues past Litton to Halton Gill before climbing over the moorland pass and the shoulder of Pen-y-ghent into Ribblesdale (see page 136).

Above Amerdale Dub the main valley of Wharfedale becomes a narrower, more mountainous dale, the river a faster-flowing stream. To the east the valley rises in steep, glaciated terraces, along one stretch of which the Dales Way footpath runs, providing a high-level walk with breathtaking views. In the

pasture below can be seen fine examples of lynchets, or raines – narrow ploughing terraces which provided space for a team of oxen to plough and furrow along the hillside. Oats were the principal crop grown, being hardier than wheat, more likely to ripen and less likely to rot in the short and cool Dales summer. Haverbread, or unleavened oatcake, was for many cenuturies the staple food of Dales communities. Many of the terraces were used for arable farming, from Anglo-Saxon times onwards, probably as part of an open field, crop rotation system. Enclosure and improved communications made it more economic for Dales farmers to specialise and leave cereal production to the drier and warmer lowlands.

The Dales Way descends past Scargill House before following field paths into Kettlewell. Scargill House is a Church of England retreat and conference centre, notable for its tall-roofed, Scandinavian style church a striking architectural feature in this part of the upper dale which blends in with the austere grandeur of the scenery. The house stands in its own extensive grounds which include terraced woodlands extending up the hillside.

Kettlewell

THE VILLAGE OF KETTLEWELL lies on the confluence of Cam Gill Beck, a fast-flowing moorland stream forming a deep-sided valley, and the River Wharfe. This, too, was a Norse settlement. Like other Wharfedale villages, Kettlewell owed its growth from the 17th century onwards to the lead mines in the nearby hills which, although nothing like as extensive as those on Grassington or Hebden Moors, were still capable of supporting a number of mining families. The fast-flowing streams powered waterwheels to drive ore-crushing machinery, part of which survives in the Craven Museum at Skipton.

Its isolated position spared Kettlewell the kind of rapid development which occured around many towns and villages in Victorian times, and the soft grey stone of its church, its cottages and larger houses blends perfectly with the greens and pale greys of the limestone crags and pastures, and the dark bracken and peat-covered fellsides which rise steeply all around.

The village's three inns are not so much an indication of the drinking habits of this small community as a relic of the days when Kettlewell lay on an important stage coach route. The coaches, coming from South Yorkshire and the Midlands, stayed in Kettlewell

Kettlewell is well placed for exploring this stretch of Wharfedale, with a choice of riverside walks or more strenuous routes over the high moorland. A number of guesthouses, holiday cottages and inns in the village cater for visitors.

before struggling their way across the murderously steep Park Rash road, with its 1-in-4 gradient, to Coverdale and Middleham, another important coaching town, and continuing towards Teeside and Tyneside. Though the great days of coaching only lasted around 50 years before the new railways took the trade away, Kettlewell's three inns remain, catering for new generations of car-borne visitors.

Kettlewell is a popular centre for ramblers. There is a good car park, a weekday and summer weekend bus service, shops, cafés, the pubs and a youth hostel. As well as the Dales Way, low-level riverside walks can be enjoyed back to Scargill by the riverside or to and from Starbotton using waymarked routes along both sides of the river. A variation, with splendid views and lots of wild flowers in spring, is to take the path (A) up to

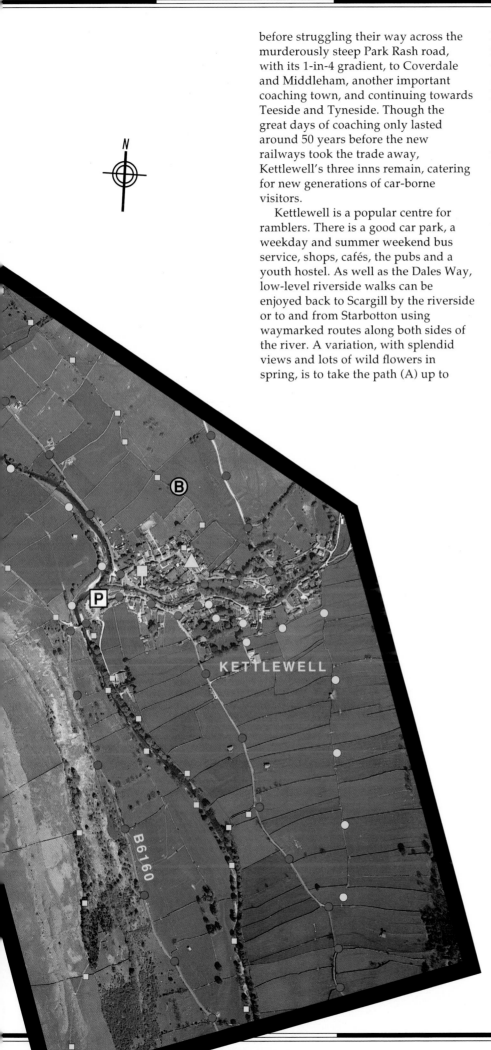

Moor End Farm before descending to Starbotton. The more energetic can take the steep green bridleway (B), which climbs out of the valley up to Cam Head, returning via Starbotton or continuing up Tor Dyke.

Tor Dyke is a remarkable Iron Age earthwork, a defensive ditch which may have been created by the Brigantian people under the command of their General, Venutius. From Tor Dyke routes can be followed across Park Rash to the summit of Great Whernside, one of the highest peaks in the Dales. This craggy, peaty summit some 2,308ft (704m) above sea level, is a superb viewpoint both across Wharfedale and down into Upper Nidderdale with its moorland reservoirs. The return can be made via Hag Dyke, or, further south, along the bridleway over Rain Slack.

Anther popular walk from Kettlewell is to follow steep paths (C) through Gate Cote Scar crags and over the summit of Old Cote Moor to Arncliffe in Littondale, perhaps returning along the valley-bottom path to Hawkswick.

Potholers, well equipped, can also enjoy good opportunities around Kettlewell. Dow Cave, a pothole with an entrance some 26ft (8m) high and 10ft (3m) wide, just off the Leyburn road, is a popular venue. It eventually leads into Dowbergill Passage, and one of the most remarkable underground features of its kind in Britain. Skilled cavers can find their way through to Providence Pot on the shoulder of Great Whernside. The cave can be dangerous and is not to be tackled without good equipment and experienced leadership.

A less strenuous way of experiencing the Dale is to take the Park Rash (Leyburn) road out of Kettlewell and, providing car and gear box are up to it, follow the 1-in-4 hairpin bends up over Scale Park. This land was granted in 1409 to the Earl of Westmorland for a warren park and hunting lodge, which gave its name to Park Rash pass. Once over the summit there follows a thrilling descent into Coverdale, passing a mysterious single standing stone, the Hunter Stone, which may have been a medieval boundary stone but also serves as a guide post which can still be of real value in mist or snowy weather. The road is often closed after snowfall, sometimes for weeks on end. Until recently this moorland pass was a gated road, but cattle grids now make it an easier road to traverse.

Starbotton

ABOVE KETTLEWELL, Upper
Wharfedale is a classic U-shaped
glaciated valley, the steep valley sides
carved out by the erosive action of the
Wharfedale glacier, and the valley
bottom flat and, in places, ill-drained,
with the river meandering between
shallow banks of boulder clay and
glacial waste.

In fact the river often bursts its banks
in this section of the valley, especially
when, in late winter, snows are melting
on the higher fells. The river rises with
great speed and covers adjacent water
meadows. Sometimes, during a long,
wet winter, fields will be under water
for weeks, almost giving the impression
of ancient, glacial lakes created along
the valley floor. When the water does
recede, it leaves tide marks of mud,
straw, branches and leaves like an
extended rim. It is often possible, well
into spring, to see clumps of straw or
leaves high in the branches of a
riverside alder or willow indicating the
height of the winter flood.

Fortunately the villages of Upper

Harry Smith, the long-serving former Secretary and Chairman of the West Riding Ramblers' Association.

There are some magnificent hill walks to be had from Starbotton. Perhaps the most impressive of these is along the ancient Walden Road (A), a bridlepath which crosses the watershed over the southern end of Buckden Pike before descending into Walden, West Burton and Wensleydale. Another steep but rewarding fell path (B), once, incredible as it might seem, reputedly used by Dales postmen, climbs over Old Cote Moor to Arncliffe. The views from this track across both Upper Wharfedale and Littondale are truly magnificent. There are also less strenuous riverside routes back to Kettlewell; the path to the east (C) climbs above the meadows and crosses a number of stiles along a raised terrace.

North of Starbotton the Dales Way continues along the left bank of the river to follow an ancient enclosed path before entering, at Birks Wood, the Upper Wharfedale estate, an area of woodland, valley and fell country extending almost to the summit of Buckden Pike and including most of Langstrothdale. This magnificent estate was recently given to the National Trust by Mr Graham Watson, a leading conservationist. Here the estate is notable for its exotic trees, including tall pines and redwoods. Many are not native to the Dales.

Wharfedale lie well above the flood line, though Starbotton, which, like Kettlewell, also lies at the confluence of the Wharfe and Cam Gill Beck, suffered a disastrous flood in 1686. When after a freak storm and huge cloudburst, not only was the Wharfe in torrent, but Cam Gill Beck rose with alarming speed and eventually overwhelmed the entire village. The disaster became nationally known and relief came from all over England – a remarkable fact considering the lack of communications at that time. Starbotton was rebuilt, and datestones on some of the cottages indicate that they pre-date the flood and were therefore restored.

Starbotton's name indicates that it was an area of woodland, probably alongside the river, where the trees were coppiced to make 'stannards' or standards (poles). The modern village is compact, and relatively quiet, with no shop or car park; only an inn, the Fox and Hounds. There are, however, some delightful cottages with colourful gardens.

The Dales Way passes Starbotton along the far side of the river, but a narrow footbridge, to the south, links the west side of the river with the village. Recently restored, this bridge is dedicated to the memory of the late

Starbotton (above and right) lies equi-distant from Kettlewell to the south and Buckden to the north. Like its neighbours, the village is positioned where a tributary river joins the Wharfe from the fells to the east.

B6160

HUBBERHOLME

Dales Way

Buckden / Hubberholme

IN MEDIEVAL TIMES the top of Wharfedale and Langstrothdale (as the Upper Dale is known beyond Buckden) formed part of Langstrothdale Chase, a Norman hunting forest celebrated for its red deer, wild boar and wolves. It was owned by the great Northumbrian family of Percy.

The village of Buckden was one of ten hunting lodges in the forest, and its name means literally 'the wood of the buck (or deer)'. The Percy foresters who lived here had the duty of imposing the strict Forest Law to protect the deer, which could mean death or imprisonment for poachers.

There is a shop and an inn, bed and breakfast accommodation and even an outdoor centre for trainee police officers here. A large National Park car park makes this a popular centre for walkers, particularly to the summit of Buckden Pike, at 2302ft (702m) the second highest peak in Wharfedale. From its high, narrow ridge is a breathtaking viewpoint not only along the valley but

across the adjacent fells, most of them long, flat topped and treeless, and all at a similar height of 2,000 – 2,300ft (650 – 700m) above sea level.

At the southern tip of the Pike is a curious monument – a small bronze cross at the base of which is an effigy of a fox. This is a memorial to five Polish airman flying for the RAF who, in January 1942, crashed in mist and lost their lives on Buckden Pike. The sixth, the survivor, was guided from the summit by a fox to the safety of the village. After the war he placed the monument there as a tribute to his friends and to the fox who had saved his life.

The track (A) northwards out of Buckden car park is no ordinary farm road but a Roman road, Julius Agricola's campaigning road which ran between his military forts at Ilkley and Bainbridge. It can be followed not only along part of Kidstones Pass, but as an unmetalled road over the Stake Pass to Semerwater and Bainbridge.

Cray is a little hamlet reached by a path branching down from this track or along the main Aysgarth road. The

Hubberholme Church is known for the interior carvings in oak by Robert Thompson of Kilburn. Thompson has become famous for the 'mouse signature' which is incorporated in all his work.

White Lion Inn is a popular walkers' pub, and lies on a choice of beautiful paths into Langstrothdale. One route goes down Cray Gill past waterfalls and a little bridge to join the lane into Hubberholme; another follows the moor edge above the Hubberholme Wood to enjoy panoramic views down the whole of Upper Wharfedale past Scar House to Hubberholme or Yockenthwaite.

Hubberholme, also on the Dales Way, is a Norse settlement. The little Church of St Michael almost certainly occupies an Anglo-Viking pagan site, and has a Norman tower and a simple interior. What is remarkable is that it has one of the last carved rood lofts in northern England, dating from 1558. Because of its remote position it survived the onslaughts of the 17th-century Puritans who destroyed such 'idolatry'. The ashes of the Yorkshire playwright, novelist, essayist and broadcaster J B Priestley are scattered here.

Just across Hubberholme's ancient bridge is the George, which, like many older inns in the Dales, once belonged to the church. Until recently, the rent of a pasture behind the church was auctioned off each New Year's Eve to local farmers, and used for the good of the poor of the parish.

Langstrothdale is a narrow, mountain valley, the River Wharfe being no more than a vigorous stream. In 'The Reeve's Tale', Geoffrey Chaucer described 'Strother', where the students Alan and John came from, as being 'farre in the north can I not tell where'. Farmsteads are scattered, Viking-style, along the dale – all of them with Norse names: Raisgill, Yockenthwaite, Deepdale, Beckermonds. The Dales Way, heading for Cam Fell, the source of the Wharfe, follows the riverside footpath between them. Just beyond Yockenthwaite there is a Bronze Age stone circle by the path, suggesting that this pass through the heart of the Pennines has been in use for some time. Energetic fell walkers have a choice of magnificent, if strenuous, routes between Langstrothdale and Upper Littondale. A bridleway crosses the fell from Redmire, to the west of Buckden Bridge, and climbs over Old Cote Moor to Litton, whilst another ancient monastic way, Horse Head Pass, climbs up Hagg Beck Gill and over the moorland summit to Halton Gill. A third fine fell path links Beckermonds with Halton Gill over Eller Carr and Great Pasture.

Early Settlement

IN ABOUT 1,000BC early huntsmen began to cross northern England in search of game, eventually working their way into the hostile Pennines and finding that the dry, limestone uplands of the Yorkshire Dales, with their less dense woodland, were relatively easy to penetrate, while the caves provided useful shelter. At Victoria Cave, near Settle, carved antler tools and weapons have been found dating from the end of the early Stone Age period, together with the bones of earlier mammoth, hippo and rhino who flourished in the area in the warmer inter-glacial period.

The Mesolithic hunters who roamed the area some 2,000 years later left traces of their activity in the form of flint tools, scrapers and flint barbs, and in upland campsites around Malham Tarn and Tan Hill in Swaledale. But it was the following generations of Neolithic peoples, the first farmers, who began to make significant changes to the Dales landscape by clearing woodland for their grazing animals and creating small arable fields, a process which greatly increased during Bronze Age times from around 2500BC when an increased population caused yet more forest to be cleared for crops such as cereal and flax. Many early

Above: The ancient cairns of Nine Standard Rigg. Their origin is unknown.

Left: Yockenthwaite stone circle in Langstrothdale.

Top right: Hut circles discernible on the summit of Ingleborough.

Right: Traces of an Iron Age settlement at Dew Bottoms.

fine example at Bainbridge, in Wensleydale, where the outline of a Roman fort can still be seen, strategically situated on a glacial drumlin.

But it was the Anglo-Saxon tribes who, in the 7th century, came from North Germany to clear and drain the impenetrable forest and swamp of the valley floors. They settled mainly in the more fertile eastern dales, probably eventually co-exisitng with the Celts to create the characteristic nucleated farming villages whose names, ending in -ley, -ham and -ton still betray their origin. Successive invasions over the next three centuries, first by Danes from the east and then by Vikings who came from the west via Ireland, added to the complex Germanic-Scandinavian mix. Danish place names, ending in -by and -thorpe, and Viking names ending in -thwaite, -set or -scale abound.

Typically, Anglo-Danish settlements in a dale – itself an old Germanic word related to the modern German word 'tal', meaning deep place or valley – form a string of small villages with farms actually within the villages, whilst dales settled by the Vikings consist of more scattered farmsteads focusing on one single, larger village.

Many hamlets and farms in the Dales have been continuously occupied from this period, and when exploring the Dales we are looking at settlement patterns that have remained relatively unchanged for a thousand years or more.

henge monuments in the Dales, including stone circles at Bordley, Malhamdale and in Langstrothdale, date from this period, as do the round and long barrows in Wharfedale and Swaledale.

The Iron Age saw the emergence in the Dales and West Yorkshire of a powerful confederation of Celtic tribes known as the Brigantes. There was extensive arable and pastoral farming of the higher, drier slopes and it is still possible to trace the outlines of Iron Age communities on the limestone pasture above Grassington and Conistone in Wharfedale, above Malham village and in Swaledale, whilst the remains of several important defensive fortifications can be seen at Tor Dyke, in Wharfedale, at Maiden Castle, in Swaledale, and on the summit of Ingleborough, an immense Celtic hillfort.

The purpose of such fortifications is obscure, but may well have been linked to the Roman invasion. The Brigantes were finally defeated around 74AD after the Battle of Stanwick, but they were perhaps never completely subdued, requiring a complex stystem of military roads and forts to be built by the Romans to keep them under control. There is a

Early Settlement

Airedale

NO INDUSTRIAL RIVER in the world can have a more unlikely origin than the Aire. It runs past the warehouses, wharves and waterfronts of Leeds, and slides past industrial Castleford, carrying huge barges of coal, oil and steel along the canalised section of the Aire-Calder Navigation. But it begins its life as a mountain river, high on Malham Moor in the limestone country of Craven.

Airedale is synonymous with the old West Riding; the home of the woollen industry, textiles, heavy engineering, Yorkshire pudding, and, of course, the little tousle-haired Airedale terrier. But the top end of Airedale, beyond Skipton, has a very different character. Here the Aire is little more than a stream, not prone to sudden floods, as are the Wharfe and Swale. If you ignore the stream which seeps its way under the bottom of Malham Cove, its main source, at Airehead Springs above Kirkby Malham, is an underground spring surging from subterranean limestone caves and passageways. The scenery is for the most part gentle: the round, green drumlins of the Aire Gap, the soft, fertile uplands around Airton and Kirkby Malham which are really foothills rather than true Dales fell country.

Yet immediately beyond Malham Cove the landscape is pure theatre; crag, cove, scar, chasm, cave, waterfall, slopes rising up at impossible angles, ravines that seem created by a fevered imagination, rather than by accident of nature.

Left: Skipton, one the Dales' main towns. Its Norman castle is remarkably well preserved.

Above: Malham Tarn and the classic limestone scenery of Malham Moor.

Right: The village of Airton, north-west of Skipton.

AIREDALE

Skipton

SKIPTON'S DUAL DEVELOPMENT, as a medieval market town and as an industrial centre, can still be traced in its physical layout. It was almost certainly a small Anglo-Saxon market or trading centre dealing in sheep, as the name 'Skip' or 'Sheep' recalls. Indeed, the lower part of the High Street is still known as Sheep Street.

Because of their strategic position in the Aire Gap, one of the few low-level passes through the Central Pennines,

William the Conqueror gave the extensive lands in Craven, formerly owned by the Saxon Earl Edwin, to Robert de Romille, a Norman adventurer and ally, and permitted him to build a castle at Skipton to defend the vital trade route. Romille's great castle still stands on a limestone crag, exploiting the natural defensive position above Eller Gill Beck. During Norman and Plantagenet times it was built up to become the stronghold of the Clifford family who played a major role in the

history of England. Immediately to the north of the castle lies the Old Park, now bisected by the Skipton northern by-pass. It was from here that Cromwell's soldiers fired canon balls at the castle walls in a long siege between 1642 and 1645.

The very layout of Skipton reflects its former function as a town and administrative centre serving the castle. The medieval church – where many of the Cliffords lie buried in elaborate tombs – is close by. The High Street runs downhill and is overlooked by the castle; it is still the site of a bustling market, and has been since the days of the Cliffords. Many of the long, narrow plots belonging to the medieval houses along the High Street were in later ages developed into courtyards, around which workshops and houses were crammed. Many of these survive, now as attractive pedestrianised shopping courts and walkways.

The Industrial Revolution came to Skipton not because of the River Aire (which is situated some distance from the town), but with the building of the Leeds-Liverpool Canal in 1773. Its Spring Branch, which still flows round the town centre and behind the castle walls, carried vast quantities of limestone down to the heart of the West Riding for iron- and later steel-making. The canal also brought cheap coal and raw materials from the Aire valley and Liverpool for the large steam-powered mills. These were much more efficient than the water-powered mills of the higher Dales, and soon dominated the market. Because it was easily linked to Lancashire via the Leeds-Liverpool Canal and the Lancashire and Yorkshire Railway, and because it enjoyed a similar mild, damp climate, Skipton became as important for cotton spinning as for wool combing and weaving. Until recently, Dewhurst's massive mill on Broughton Road manufactured high-quality sewing cottons.

Skipton grew rapidly during the last century from its compact medieval core around the central High Street to a medium-sized industrial town, as mills and factories were built alongside the canal and railway, and low-cost terraced housing was constructed for the workers along the canal and main roads to the south.

In the second half of the 20th century, administration and service industries – such as local government, education, tourism, shopping and the Skipton Building Society – have replaced much of the textile industry, and newer estates of semi-detached houses now spread up the hillsides around the town. New by-passes now carry much of the through-traffic away from the town centre, but because of Skipton's continuing strategic position as a tourist and shopping centre, within a short drive of the large South Lancashire and West Yorkshire conurbations, traffic congestion in its narrow streets remains a problem. The town also enjoys an excellent, frequent rail service from Leeds and Bradford, soon to be electrified.

Skipton Castle, largely restored in the 17th century, is one of finest and best preserved castles in the North of England. Particularly fascinating are Conduit Court, and the antechamber covered with tropical shells collected by George Clifford, Duke of Cumberland, an Elizabethan sailor and adventurer. The castle is open daily. The Craven Museum, in the neo-Georgian Town Hall, is devoted to Dales' natural, local and industrial history, including lead-mining.

Gargrave

BETWEEN SKIPTON and Gargrave lies one of the most dramatic sections of the Aire Gap, where river, canal, turnpike road, modern trunk road and railway all share a narrow valley bottom, barely half a mile wide. To the north is Sharp Haw, the first of the high, gritstone-capped peaks of the Dales, a fine viewpoint and popular walk from Skipton.

To the south is a series of rolling drumlins – smooth grassy hillocks of glacial waste – which lie like gigantic eggs in a huge basket, filling the Aire Gap, around which river, road and railway have to squeeze their way. The drumlins gradually give way to the higher, gritstone moors of the South Pennines, rising to Pinhaw Beacon, another noted viewpoint and one of the Tudor chain of ancient bonfire sites, which brought news of such events as the coming of the Spanish Armada.

The 127-mile (203km) long Leeds-Liverpool Canal was the first trans-Pennine waterway, which reached as far as Holmbridge, west of Gargrave, from Leeds by 1777. For another 39 years this remained its western terminus, owing to financial problems caused by the Napoleonic Wars; the canal was finally completed, extending to Liverpool Docks, in 1816.

Unlike later canals across the Pennines, the Leeds-Liverpool is a 'broad' canal, capable of taking vessels up to 14ft (4m) wide as opposed to the 7ft (2m) of a 'narrow' canal, and up to 60ft (18m) long. It is also a contour canal, exploiting the natural features of the landscape. Nowhere is this better demonstrated than west of Gargrave where the canal makes a series of extraordinary loops to avoid locks or expensive viaducts. Now exclusively a leisure waterway, the Leeds-Liverpool Canal provides boating, angling and walking along its towpath, and is a haven of wildlife; it also retains many impressive architectural features, incuding locks with much of the original machinery still intact.

Gargrave owes much of its present size to both road and canal transport. Because it lay on the important Keighley-Kendal turnpike road, its large coaching inns, such as the White Swan, catered for the needs of stage coach passengers and the servicing of horses. Its wharves and warehouses along the canal carried lead and zinc from Wharfedale and Malhamdale mines, and brought coal into the area. There were even passenger boats to Blackburn in the 1820s and '30s, before the opening of the 'Little' North-Western Railway, with its links to Skipton, Hellifield and Ingleton.

Further transport development will occur when the A65 trunk road, currently following the old Keighley-Kendal turnpike road, will be taken out of the village centre and along a new bypass.

Modern Gargrave, set away from the busy main road, is a quiet, mainly residential village. To the east of the town is Johnson & Johnson's factory, with its tall chimney, a local landmark. Medical supplies and baby products are manufactured there; the site was chosen because of the clean air of the Yorkshire Dales.

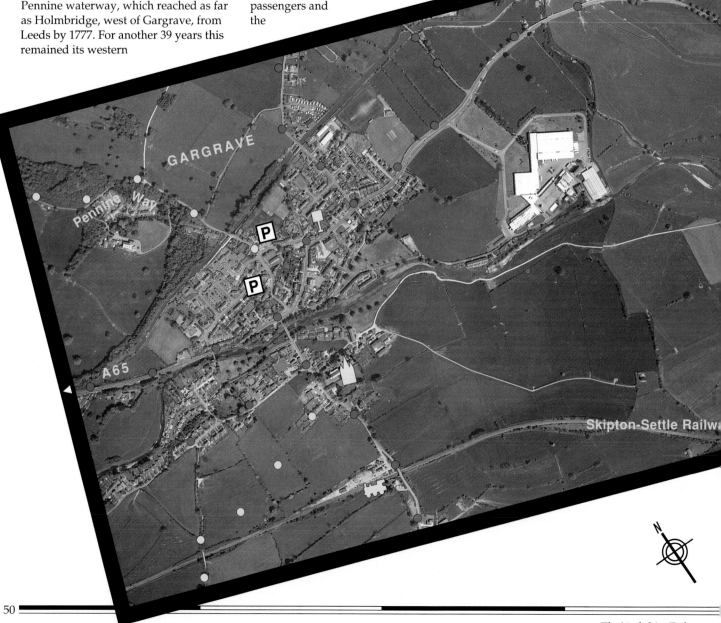

Buses and trains link the village with Skipton and Leeds. Shops and cafés cater for local people and visitors, including walkers and cyclists. The River Aire is here a sparkling stream, flowing through the quiet village green, rather than the polluted waterway it becomes by the time it reaches Leeds and the Lower Aire valley. The church, rebuilt in 1852, has retained its 15th-century tower, and fragments of Anglo-Saxon crosses indicate its older origin. In the churchyard lies a former Chancellor of the Exchequer, the late Ian McCleod, who served in Edward Heath's administration in 1970.

About a ½ mile(800m) east of Gargrave, in a field close to the railway line, is the site of a Roman villa with a courtyard, one of the few to be recorded in the Yorkshire Dales, reflecting the hostility of the area both in terms of climate and the local population. As the villa was destroyed, probably violently, some time during the 3rd century, it would

seem that such caution was amply justified.

In addition to the Pennine Way, which goes through the centre of the village, there are good walks into Malhamdale, back to Skipton via Sharp Haw summit or

Crag Wood planation, and to Bell Busk, Otterburn and Hellfield. It is also possible to go southwards along the meandering Leeds-Liverpool towpath, between the attractive rolling green drumlins, to East Marton and Thornton-in-Craven.

Gargrave

Airedale

Coniston Cold / Bell Busk

ON ITS 250-MILE (400km) journey from Edale in the Peak District to Kirk Yetholm in Scotland, the Pennine Way goes through Gargrave and past Gargrave Park before heading westwards along Mark House Lane, north-west of the village. This is an old packhorse route, in use as the main road to Settle before the present road and turnpike were built. It soon leaves the road to bear northwards through more drumlins and scattered copses, passing Heber Hill, Harrow Hill and Haw Crag to Eshton Moor, with fine views across to Malhamdale as the path ascends the low hills.

The Pennine Way was the first of Britain's long-distance footpaths (now known as national trails), and was established in 1965. It owes its origins to

Bank Newton, on the Leeds-Liverpool Canal west of Gargrave, is a centre for canal cruising.

an article by Tom Stephenson in the *Daily Herald* in 1938 which suggested a 'long green trail', running along the crests of hills through the North of England, rather like the Appalachian Way in North America, which was in turn based on the pioneering waymarked long-distance trails in the Black Forest of Germany. World War II prevented any action on Stephenson's suggestion, but following the 1949 National Parks and Access to the Countryside Act, the Pennine Way was formally established, using existing ancient green ways and public paths for most of its length.

West of Gargrave, the River Aire and the Leeds-Liverpool Canal, which have kept company from Leeds, separate. The canal swings southwards and ascends six flights of locks, through rolling countryside of pastureland and scattered woodland, towards the Lancashire border and Foulridge Tunnel. The river turns northwards into Malhamdale. Beyond Newton Lock at Bank Newton, a popular canal cruising centre west of Gargrave, is the 6-mile (9.6km) long summit pound of the canal, some 463ft (143m) above sea level. Water for the summit pound comes along a 9-mile (14km) long aqueduct from Winterburn Reservoir north of Gargrave, a remarkable feature of early 19th-century engineering. The reservoir was built purely to serve the needs of the waterway.

Coniston Cold, along the main road, is a small estate village serving Coniston Hall, with its extensive landscaped parkland, woodlands and lake (no public access), visible from the main road which crosses the edge of the park.

Further north is the hamlet of Bell Busk. Its curious name may come from an inn sign – a 'busk' or 'bush' was the medieval sign of an inn, and the Bell was probably the name of the inn. The inn, if it ever existed, has long since vanished, but as the lane along which Bell Busk is situated used to be the main waggon and packhorse way to Kendal (before the Keighley-Kendal turnpike road was built in the 1760s), this is a likely explanation. Nothing now remains but a few farms and cottages. A ruined farmhouse on the hilltop overlooking the lane is still known as Kendal Hill.

For many years, however, Bell Busk had a railway station which only closed in the late 1950s as rail traffic declined in favour of more direct buses and cars. The station buildings, in typical 'Little North-Western Railway' half-timbered style, survive as a private house. Known as 'Bell Busk for Malham' in all the timetables, this was in fact the principal station for Malham village, and in former times waggonettes would arrive at the station to take excursionists there. Cyclists and walkers would take the more direct green track via Well Head to Airton and Malham village, still a delightful walk.

A fine walk from Gargrave via Bell Busk leads to Otterburn to join Langber Lane, the ancient Kendal road to Settle, which for most of its route is a grassy or stony track cutting along the edge of the high fells before descending into Settle. Alternatively, there is an attractive valley and moorland route northwards from Otterburn, crossing the Airton road before finally emerging at Kirkby Malham church.

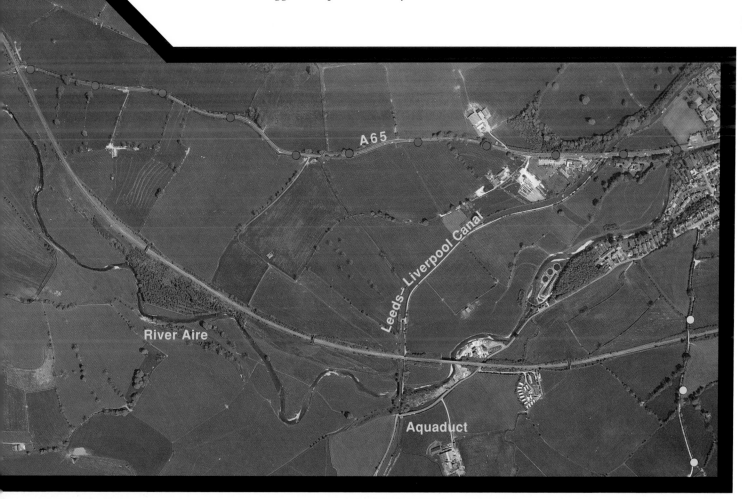

Calton / Airton

AT THE POINT WHERE the River Aire swings northwards beyond Bell Busk, its valley narrows and assumes the name Malhamdale. The green track from Bell Busk soon passes Well Head Laithe, the site of an old spring, one of many in this part of the Dales where streams, having run underground from limestone sink holes, follow impervious aquafers to emerge as well heads or springs in fields some miles away. 'Laithe' is a common dialect word, of Norse origin, used throughout the Dales for a barn or cow-house.

Kirk Syke Lane, as the track is known beyond Well Head, passes the reputed site of another Roman villa, not far from the present Kirk Syke farm. The name Kirk Syke indicates that this may have been used for Christian workship before the church at Kirkby Malham was built.

The Pennine Way joins the River Aire at a footbridge by Eel Ark Hill and continues alongside the river all the way to Malham. Newfield Hall, on the hillside to the east, lies in its own parkland and ornamental woods. This handsome Edwardian country mansion belonged for some years to the Holiday Fellowship, and is now used as an HF Youth and Education Centre.

Airton is a striking village, with several attractive 17th- and 18th-century houses situated around an unusual triangular village green upon which there is a single cottage – a clear but unusual example of encroachment on the green, a practice normally strongly resisted by villagers. To the south of the green is one of the earliest Friends' Meeting Houses in this part of the Dales, dated 1700.

A short way along the lane westwards towards Settle is Airton's twin hamlet of Scosthrop. Its name suggests that it may have been a settlement of Danes or Vikings who, by agreement with the original Anglian settlers in Airton, created their own community close by. The term 'Scots' or 'Scottas' was used by Anglo-Saxons for any outsiders; the word 'throp' establishes their Norse identity. Scosthrop Manor is a lovely early Jacobean farmouse, dated 1686 on its porch but 1603 on an inner doorway.

Airton's water-powered mill collected river water which was carried by goit or leat – mill race – from a weir to the north. This built up a sufficient head of water to drive an overshot waterwheel in typical Pennine fashion. The mills situated by the bridge on the Calton road, was one of several small textile mills in Mahamdale

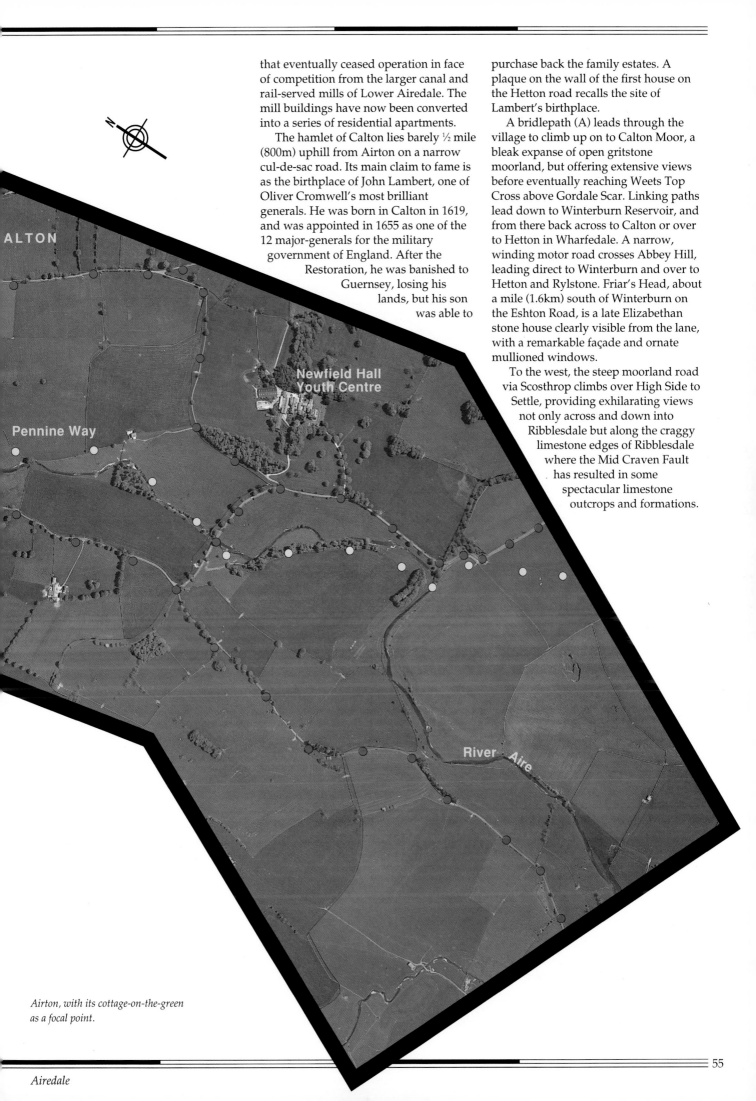

that eventually ceased operation in face of competition from the larger canal and rail-served mills of Lower Airedale. The mill buildings have now been converted into a series of residential apartments.

The hamlet of Calton lies barely ½ mile (800m) uphill from Airton on a narrow cul-de-sac road. Its main claim to fame is as the birthplace of John Lambert, one of Oliver Cromwell's most brilliant generals. He was born in Calton in 1619, and was appointed in 1655 as one of the 12 major-generals for the military government of England. After the Restoration, he was banished to Guernsey, losing his lands, but his son was able to purchase back the family estates. A plaque on the wall of the first house on the Hetton road recalls the site of Lambert's birthplace.

A bridlepath (A) leads through the village to climb up on to Calton Moor, a bleak expanse of open gritstone moorland, but offering extensive views before eventually reaching Weets Top Cross above Gordale Scar. Linking paths lead down to Winterburn Reservoir, and from there back across to Calton or over to Hetton in Wharfedale. A narrow, winding motor road crosses Abbey Hill, leading direct to Winterburn and over to Hetton and Rylstone. Friar's Head, about a mile (1.6km) south of Winterburn on the Eshton Road, is a late Elizabethan stone house clearly visible from the lane, with a remarkable façade and ornate mullioned windows.

To the west, the steep moorland road via Scosthrop climbs over High Side to Settle, providing exhilarating views not only across and down into Ribblesdale but along the craggy limestone edges of Ribblesdale where the Mid Craven Fault has resulted in some spectacular limestone outcrops and formations.

Airton, with its cottage-on-the-green as a focal point.

Scalegill
Mill

Ⓐ

Kirkby Malham / Hanlith

THE ROAD FROM AIRTON passes
Skellands House before descending
sharply to Kirkby Malham, situated on a
crossroads in the narrow valley formed
by Kirkby Beck. Skellands was the home
of Dr James King, who accompanied
Captain Cooke on his pioneering voyages
around the world. He wrote an account
of the journey, but died in 1784 at the
early age of 31.

Kirkby Malham has a venerable
church, probably established in Anglo-
Saxon times, but later destroyed by the
Danes. The dedication to St Michael was
often given to Christianise a Pagan site.
The name Kirkby Malham combines
Danish and Anglo-Saxon elements,
suggesting its discovery and renaming
by Danish settlers. Like many other
ancient church sites in the Dales, it was
situated well away from the communities
it originally served. The present village
remains extremely small, little more than
a handful of cottages and an inn.
However, the ecclesiastical parish is one
of the largest in the Dales, covering the
whole of Malhamdale in an area
extending from Otterburn in the south to
the whole of Malham Moor.

The present church dates from the 15th
century but it was largely rebuilt in the last
century, though a Norman font remains,
as does the ancient south door with an
'invasion beam' that could be drawn
across to help defend the villagers against
marauding Scots. Particularly intriguing
are two worn stone heads, in the north
arcade. These are probably Celtic heads,
fairly common in the Dales; they were
often placed near wells or springs to

Ⓑ

HANLITH

Hanlith
Bridge

Pennine Way

KIRKBY
MALHAM

River Aire

Although now little more than a hamlet, Kirkby Malham has a church that indicates the extent of the original parish.

symbolise magic powers and eternal life: a ritualisation of the use of the severed heads of enemies for the same purpose. Like many Pagan traditions, such superstition lingered on in country areas to be absorbed into folk custom, and even into religion.

Another fascinating feature is the signature of Oliver Cromwell in the parish register, recording his witnessing of a wedding in 1655 whilst staying with General Lambert at nearby Calton. A tiny stream runs through the old churchyard, and if you look carefully you can find the twin graves of a husband and wife, buried in the last century and separated by the fast-flowing stream.

The village of Kirkby Malham occupies an important niche in the history of the British National Park movement. It was in a cottage on the Malham road that John Dower wrote his major report on the future of National Parks during the last years of the War. That document – the Dower Report – became the basis of the 1949 National Park and Access to the Countryside Act,

establishing the Yorkshire Dales and ten other areas of the finest countryside in England and Wales as National Parks.

Kirkby Malham's twin hamlet of Hanlith lies at the other side of the River Aire across Hanlith Bridge. On the hillside overlooking the river is Hanlith Hall, a 17th-century manor house which has been remodelled three times. It has a richly decorated doorway with a halberd carved on each side. A track (A), Windy Pike Lane, leads up from the hamlet on to Hanlith Moor, a typical moorland 'outgang' or access road giving common right holders a right of passage with their stock onto the high fells. The track eventually leads to Weets Cross and joins the bridlepath from Calton.

Kirk Gill Wood, immediately to the west of Kirkby Malham, lies on the higher Yoredale limestones and contains a mineral spring. It is also noted for its wildflowers in spring. The road westwards out of Kirkby Malham, Cow Close Lane, climbs Grains Bridge to join the Airton road over High Side to Settle.

Attractive footpaths follow the riverside from Airton, northwards into Malham through pastures dotted with mature chesnut and sycamore trees. The Pennine Way takes the west bank, going through Hanlith before descending to the river, whilst the path (B) along the east bank passes Scalegill Mill, once the manorial corn mill, and later used for flax- and cotton-spinning. It is now used for residential accommodation, but the weir, goit and mill pond survive, still powering a hydro-electric turbine, which provides power for the complex.

Further along, the path bears round the outside of Aire Head Springs, surging up from beneath the ground. This is the point where the stream which flows out of the Malham Tarn, and disappears at Water Sinks to the south of the Tarn, reappears to join the infant River Aire. Both riverside banks are scattered with wildflowers in spring – celandines, primroses, marsh marigolds, musks and water avens, whilst dippers are usually to be seen darting from river boulders.

Malham / Malham Cove

MALHAM AND ITS immediate surroundings contain some of the most spectacular limestone scenery of the British Isles. The Mid Craven Fault, crossing above Malham village, produces several dramatic features where the Great Scar or Mountain limestone has been exposed by movement of the earth's crust and weathered into fantastic shapes.

None is more impressive than Malham Cove – a vast, crescent-shaped cliff of pale limestone, streaked with lichen stains, some 650ft (200m) long and 286ft (70m) high in the centre. Three narrow ledges run around the cliff face, the lowest negotiable (with care) on foot, whilst a stream seeps from the base of the cliff. This stream comes from becks around Capon Hall and Fountain Fell to form part of the source of the River Aire. At least part of Malham Cove is the base of a former huge waterfall, enhanced by the action of surface springs and some cave collapse. Glaciers probably removed much of the rock fall at the base of the face. In later years, the water found its way down various sink holes through fissures in the limestone, leaving a dry valley above. It is recorded that water last

Malham Cove, probably one of the most spectacular and well-known classic limestone features in England.

flowed over the rim of the Cove in 1775 and 1824 when, after floods, the Tarn overflowed and mud and debris blocked the sink holes, forcing the waters over the edge of the Cove to recreate the gigantic waterfall.

A well-surfaced path – the Pennine Way – links the Cove with Malham village, and stone steps lead up the side of the Cove to the limestone pavements on its summit. These occur where exposed limestone has been weathered to smooth 'clints' divided by deep ravines or 'grykes', in which hart's tongue fern and herb robert flourish. They need to be negotiated with great care. Some of the finest examples of limestone pavement in the British Isles are to be seen in the Malham area. The Pennine Way crosses this pavement above the Cove to make its way up to the Tarn along a monastic track, Trougate.

From the top of the Cove, and elsewhere between the Cove and Gordale Scar, some of the most remarkable early field systems in England can be seen, grassy mounds indicating the outlines of Celtic fields, over which are imposed medieval field patterns and late 18th century enclosures. Evening or winter sunshine, or even light snowfall expose these features most vividly, together with

Malham village, linked to the Cove by a footpath, inevitably becomes very crowded during the tourist season. Despite this, it remains unspoilt.

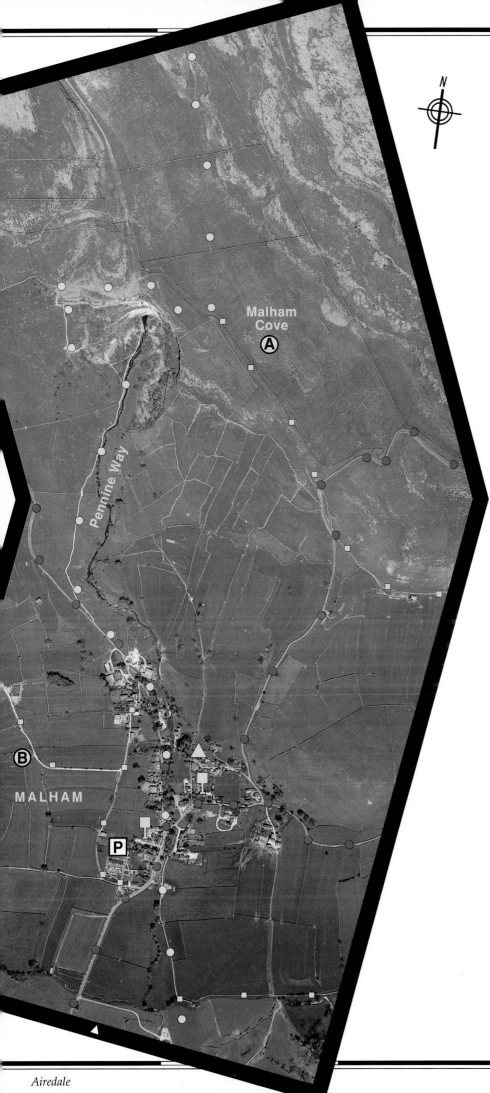

Malham Cove

Pennine Way

(A)

(B)

MALHAM

P

the lines of lynchets – ploughing terraces – which may themselves be up to a thousand years old.

Gordale Scar, about a mile (1.6km) to the east, and linked by a fieldpath (A), rivals even the Cove for dramatic effect. Gordale is an immense yet narrow gorge, caused by the meltwaters of another ancient glacial lake, with walls some 160ft (50m) high, yet barely 50ft (15m) across at its narrowest place. It was long regarded as one of the wonders of England, visited by poets, painters and travel writers. The stream which cascades down the narrow gorge has, over the centuries, deposited tufa, a hard calcium carbonate rock-like deposit formed from the precipitate of the lime-rich water. Unfortunately, heavy foot erosion has in recent years worn away much of the tufa, and visitors are requested not to climb the waterfalls.

The streamside footpath from Gordale down to Malham village goes past Janet's Foss, a waterfall which has created a broad apron of tufa as it spills into a bowl-shaped pool. A small cave overlooks the waterfall and pool. The path continues through ash woods to join the Pennine Way just south of Malham village.

A typical Anglian farming settlement, the village of Malham was divided in monastic times between two landowners: the canons of Bolton Priory and the monks of Fountains Abbey, who established the great sheepwalks on Malham Moor. In the 18th century, lead, copper and calamine were smelted from ores won from moorland mines along the fault line, whilst textile mills flourished alongside the river.

Because of the fame of its limestone scenery, Malham has long been a busy tourist village, with a large car park and National Park centre. Yet despite the crowds, the village remains relatively unspoiled, with a number of 17th- and 18th-century farmhouses and cottages around a small green, and a hump-backed bridge over the river. There is a choice of cafés, outdoor and souvenir shops, two pubs, a youth hostel and a bus service, and whilst most people follow the busy path to the Cove and Gordale Scar, other paths from the village are far less heavily used: for example, to Pikedaw Hill (B), with its calamine (zinc) mines along the line of the Craven Fault, or across to Accraplatts and Kirkby Malham. A particularly good route follows the old green road westwards from the Cove road, north of the Cove, and climbs past Nappe Cross and Kirkby Fell to Stackhouse for Settle.

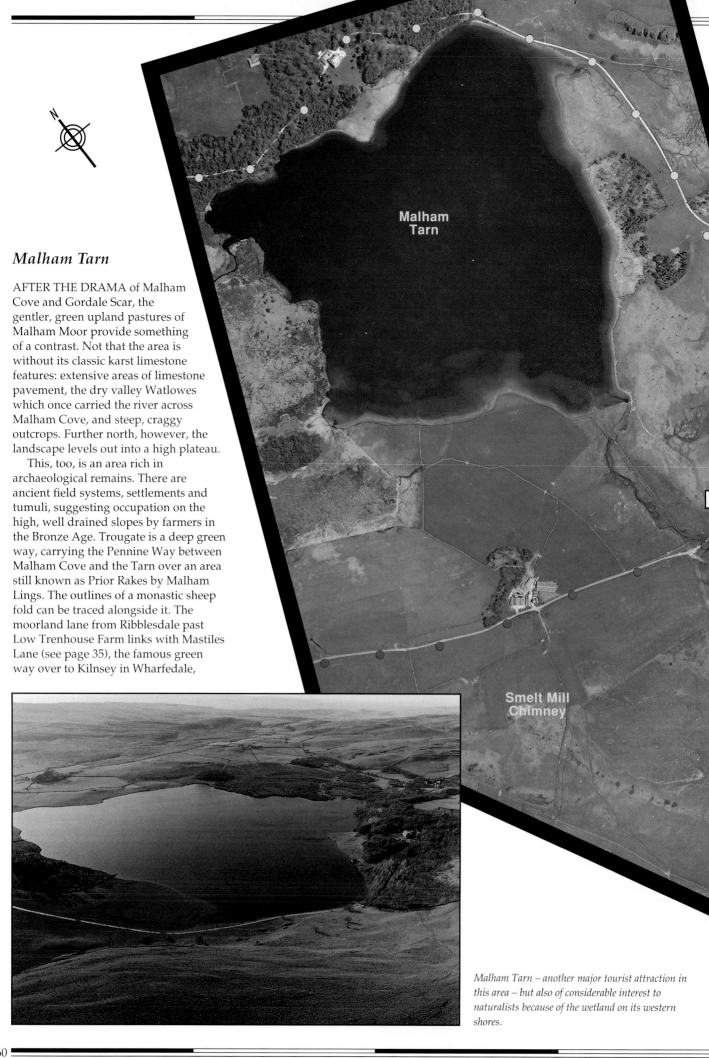

Malham Tarn

AFTER THE DRAMA of Malham
Cove and Gordale Scar, the
gentler, green upland pastures of
Malham Moor provide something
of a contrast. Not that the area is
without its classic karst limestone
features: extensive areas of limestone
pavement, the dry valley Watlowes
which once carried the river across
Malham Cove, and steep, craggy
outcrops. Further north, however, the
landscape levels out into a high plateau.

This, too, is an area rich in
archaeological remains. There are
ancient field systems, settlements and
tumuli, suggesting occupation on the
high, well drained slopes by farmers in
the Bronze Age. Trougate is a deep green
way, carrying the Pennine Way between
Malham Cove and the Tarn over an area
still known as Prior Rakes by Malham
Lings. The outlines of a monastic sheep
fold can be traced alongside it. The
moorland lane from Ribblesdale past
Low Trenhouse Farm links with Mastiles
Lane (see page 35), the famous green
way over to Kilnsey in Wharfedale,

Malham Tarn

Smelt Mill Chimney

*Malham Tarn – another major tourist attraction in
this area – but also of considerable interest to
naturalists because of the wetland on its western
shores.*

passing the site of a small Roman camp just to the east of Gordale Beck. This may at one time have been a Roman route between Upper Wharfedale and Ribblesdale: the name Street Gate almost certainly indicates the former existence of a paved road.

The 150-acre (61ha) Malham Tarn, sheltered by a crescent of wooded hillside, dominates this area. This is one of only two natural lakes in the Yorkshire Dales, this one all the more remarkable because it appears to lie above the Great Scar limestone. In fact, this is an illusion: owing to a complex geological process, resulting from the North Craven Fault, ancient underlying, impervious Silurian slates have been forced to the surface to contain the lake. It was probably originally created by captured glacial meltwaters, lying in a hollow contained within peat and

boulder clay. In later years, the level of the lake was artificially raised by means of a small weir, to improve its use for boating and fishing by the occupants of Malham Tarn House. This Victorian mansion has a wood and boathouses on its northern shore, and is now Malham Tarn Field Centre.

Tarn Moss, the wetland to the west of the tarn, is a nature reserve of international importance, containing a complex mixture of acid peats close to limestone outcrops and woodlands. Rare orchids flourish in the marshy conditions, together with such species as grass of Parnassus, twayblades, bean bog and a huge variety of grasses. Access into the reserve is strictly limited, though there is a public path – the Pennine Way – through the woods and past the Field Studies Centre. The woods are rich in wild flowers, including bluebells, water avens and primroses. Globe Flower Wood, near the road, is, as its name implies, filled with huge clumps of this golden headed flower in late spring. The tarn itself harbours native birds including coots, mallards, moorhens, terns, grebes and also many migrants.

There is a nature trail through the woods, and serious students of botany or entomology can attend one of the Field Study Council's residential courses at Tarn House. This was once the former home of local MP and philanthropist William Morrison, whose regular guests included John Ruskin and Charles Kingsley.

Many of the scattered farms around Malham Moor, such as High and Low Trenhouse, Tennant Gill, Middle House and Darnbrook, were expanded by the monks of Fountains Abbey. Farms were managed by lay shepherds, and were administered from the granges at Malham, Bordley and Kilnsey. Crosses were placed at key points in the estate, both to mark boundaries (territorial disputes between the monks of Fountains and the canons of Bolton were common) and to act as waymarks, a function which the cross shafts at Weets and Nappa still fulfil.

Great Close, the wide pasture land east of Malham Tarn, was the site, in the 17th and 18th centuries, of regular fairs held for the sale of sheep and cattle. The livestock was brought down in vast numbers from Scotland by drovers, who would fatten their beasts on the sweet pastures after the long trek, before selling them to dealers. They were then taken to feed the populations of the growing cities of Lancashire, Yorkshire and the Midlands. Up to 5,000 head of cattle could be seen at the fair at any one time, as well as sheep and horses. There was even an ale house established close by to meet the needs of farmers and drovers during their bargaining.

Much of Malham Moor is now an area of Special Scientific Interest and is owned by the National Trust, creating a magnificent heartland in the limestone uplands of the Yorkshire Dales, now under stringent management for conservation and nature protection.

The narrow lanes that cross Malham Moor over to Littondale via Darnbrook, or to Stainforth in Ribblesdale via Henside, or to Langcliffe via Cowside, are real mountain roads that require careful navigation. The Pennine Way twists northwards past Tennant Gill farm before ascending the peaty wastes of Fountain Fell – as its name implies, once the property of Fountains Abbey. A particularly beautiful path north from Malham Tarn climbs past old farm buildings at Middle House before descending across the rocky pastures to Darnbrook. The Monk's Road, a monastic bridleway, branches off this path above Middle House before slanting its way across Yew Coggar Scar and descending into Arncliffe and Littondale.

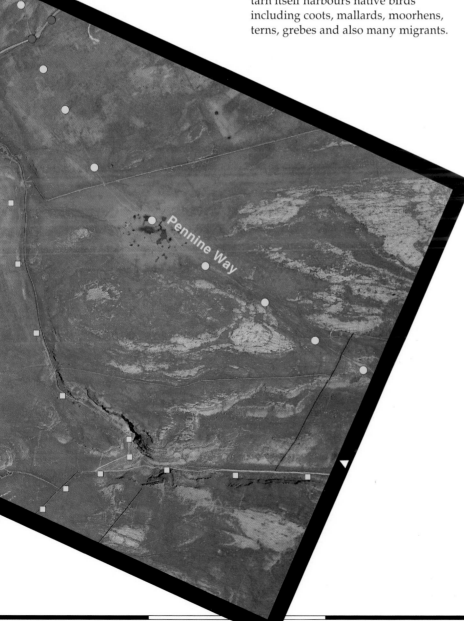

Pennine Way

Ribblesdale

RIBBLESDALE, LIKE AIREDALE, has a split personality. Its river has a thoroughly Lancashire character winding its way past some of the loveliest and most typical countryside of North Lancashire, with the county town of Preston on its banks. Yet this same river begins its life high on the peat bogs and limestone ravines in the central fells of the Yorkshire Dales, soon squeezing its way past some of Yorkshire's most famous mountain scenery.

It was Ribblesdale that led the great Victorian poet Gerard Manley Hopkins to declare: 'Earth, sweet Earth, sweet landscape with leaves throng' as he saw its wooded slopes from the grounds of Stonyhurst College. The green, meandering valley twists its way past the

Right: The market town of Settle.

Below: Pen-y-ghent, separating Ribblesdale and Littondale.

Roman fort of Ribchester and the ancient towns Whalley and Clitheroe, with the Forest of Bowland to the west and Pendle Hill to the east. It then continues past Sawley Abbey and Gisburn Park, before being deflected slightly eastwards as it approaches the massif of the Dales fell country, past the villages of Hellifield and Long Preston.

Hellifield contains the old Midland Railway Junction, where the former Lancashire & Yorkshire Railway line from Manchester, Blackburn and Preston followed Ribblesdale to meet the Midland line from Leeds coming up the Aire valley and across the Aire Gap. Its grand old station is due to be restored, and the Blackburn – Hellifield line will be reopened for regular passenger services.

Not only river, road and railway share Ribblesdale but also the Ribble Way footpath, which ascends the dale from estuary to source, using routes along or close to the riverside on its 72-mile (116km) long route between Longton, near the coast west of Preston, and the

Above: Attermire Scar, east of Settle.

Right: Road, rail and river north of Stainforth.

river's source on Gayle Moor, north of Ribblehead.

The most impressive part of the whole Dale is undoubtedly the limestone country north of Settle, where it becomes part of the National Park. However, this is also the section most affected by recent industrial activity. Major quarries, initially developed because of the easy access afforded by the railway but now entirely served by road, have created huge scars on the landscape. In spite of this, Upper Ribblesdale has a grandeur that reflects the vast scale of its surrounding fells. It also retains an intimate beauty in the many deep, secret gills that feed into the main valley, a factor that makes it one of the most individual and rewarding of the major dales.

Giggleswick, situated across the Ribble from Settle, with the green-domed chapel of its public school in the foreground.

RIBBLESDALE

Giggleswick/Langcliffe

THE TOWN OF SETTLE forms a natural gateway into Upper Ribblesdale from Lancashire and West Yorkshire. The main A65 trunk road travelling north and west no longer goes through the town which now escapes most long-distance traffic, thanks to the Settle bypass.

Settle enjoys a superb setting alongside the Ribble, overlooked by the great line of limestone crags of the Mid Craven Fault, forming what is sometimes called the Ribblesdale Edges. The most westerly of these crags, known as Castlebergh, looms over the town, and in the 18th century was used as a gigantic sundial, markings on the ground indicating its line of shadow as the hours passed. It now forms a small park, with a steep path zig-zagging up to its summit from behind the town; from the top there is a superb view across the stone rooftops of the town to its twin village of Giggleswick and across the river valley to the hills of the Forest of Bowland beyond.

A local man almost literally stumbled across the entrance to Victoria Cave in the early 19th century. Important prehistoric finds were discovered there, including human artefacts from the Old Stone Age, and these can be seen in the Museum of North Craven Life in Settle.

Settle is a town of great character. Its market square has a colourful Tuesday market (its charter granted by Henry III in 1249), drawing traders from a wide area of both Lancashire and Yorkshire. A unique feature is The Shambles, a row of double storey shops in the Market

Square, topped by a third storey of living accommodation. The town hall, formerly the offices of a Rural District Council, was built in 1832 in Elizabethan style. Narrow streets and old courtyards around the town contain some fascinating 17th-, 18th- and early 19th-century stone shops, cottages, town houses and warehouses. Outstanding among these is the Folly, just behind the market place, dating from 1679 and decorated in richly ornamental style. Several lovely Georgian houses reflect Settle's importance and prosperity in the late 18th century both as a market town and an early industrial centre. Two old inns on the main road indicate the town's role as a coaching stop on the main Keighley-Kendal turnpike, whilst the railway station on the Settle-Carlisle line is a beautifully preserved example of a small Midland railway station. Curiously enough this is not Settle's first station. Before the Settle-Carlisle line opened in 1876, Settle station was at Settle Junction, on the Lancaster line. Old textile mills by the river, formerly water-powered, date from Settle's days as a manufacturing town in the early years of the Industrial Revolution.

Two personalities are linked with Settle: George Birkbeck (1776 – 1841), son of a local banker who started the Mechanics Institute adult education movement in Britain, and Edwin Waugh (1839-1908), founder of the the National Society for the Prevention of Cruelty to Children. Edward Elgar frequently stayed

in either Giggleswick or Settle when visiting friends in Ribblesdale, and an Elgar Way footpath route visits sites connected with the composer. The excellent Museum of North Craven Life in Chapel Place explores many facets of Settle and Upper Ribblesdale's history.

Giggleswick, just across the river from Settle, lies on the long wooded ridge of Giggleswick Scar. Its 12th-century parish church, St Alkelda's, and a number of delightful 17th- and early 18th-century cottages are worth seeing. However, it is Giggleswick Public School which dominates much of the village, and in particular the green-domed, richly decorated school chapel, built on a low hillock in 1901 to the design of Thomas Jackson.

Langcliffe, to the north of Settle, is another unspoiled village, surrounding a large green with a fountain and a sycamore ringed with seats. This, too, was a mill village and Langcliffe Mill, down by the river and now on a caravan site, was originally part of an important industrial complex, entirely powered from the fast-flowing Ribble. The mill weir has a salmon leap; the Ribble has become a good salmon river.

Settle is the starting point for a wide choice of fine walks, none more impressive than the 6-mile (9.6km) high-level route to Malham that leaves the monastic track to Langcliffe off Constitution Hill and crosses to Stockdale. The path passes a vast amphitheatre of limestone crags, including Warrendale Knots and Attermire Scar, whose dolomite-like shapes and cave entrances give an impression of far greater height and magnitude than they actually have. Paths from either Settle or Langcliffe lead past the entrance to Victoria Cave, discovered in 1838 by a local man, Michael Horner, out walking his dog, and named after the young Queen. It was the site of some of the most important archaeological finds in the north of England, and is a spendid viewpoint in its own right.

Stainforth

THE 22 MILES (35km) of the Settle-Carlisle Railway, between Settle Junction and the line's summit at Aisgill, earned the name 'The Long Drag' in steam engine days, when perspiring firemen had to fire a hard-working locomotive up the 1-in-100 gradient. North of Settle, the line becomes increasingly impressive, thrusting its way past Langcliffe towards Stainforth, much of the line running along a deep cutting through the solid limestone, where, in spring, masses of primroses flourish. At Taitlands, south of Stainforth, the line goes through its first tunnel after leaving Settle, built at the insistence of a local landowner who didn't want the new railway polluting his parkland.

Robert's Papermill, the higher of the two Langcliffe mills, is the only working mill still left in the National Park, and nowadays recycles paper.

Close by, on the other side of the road, is the Hoffman Kiln. Now owned by Craven District Council, this remarkable oval limestone kiln was built in 1873 to burn limestone for quicklime and hydrated lime, used to make cement and for other purposes. The patented process allowed continuous burning around the oval kiln. Fresh coal and limestone was supplied through roof portals, and the processed lime was extracted and loaded in trucks on the adjacent Settle-Carlisle railway. The quarry is now closed and used as a tip – though part is

a nature reserve, noted for its orchids. There are plans to preserve the remains of the kiln as a major industrial monument and visitor centre.

Stainforth, as its name implies, was a stony ford across the river. It also lies above an attractive series of waterfalls, Stainforth Foss. The ford was on an important cross-Pennine packhorse route, used by the monks and their successors to carry goods by trains of packponies between the ports of Lancaster and York. In 1670 a sturdy new packhorse bridge was built by Samuel Watson of Knight Stainforth to facilitate the river crossing. Both Stainforth Foss and bridge are now in the hands of the National Trust.

Stainforth is really two villages, separated by the river. Little or Knight Stainforth, to the west of the river, includes the 17th-century Stainforth Hall, a yeoman farmer's house which is now part of a caravan site, and Stainforth or Stainforth-under-Bargh, the village at the other side of the busy bypass (an underpass links the village school with the village centre). There is a narrow main street, an old inn, a shop and post office and a solid village church, built in 1842.

Stepping stones in the village lead across Stainforth Beck into Goat Scar Lane, a continuation of the packhorse trail leading towards Malham. At the top of this steep lane, a stile leads to a path across to Catrigg Force, a narrow waterfall on Stainforth Gill in a wooded

cleft in the hillside. In its way this is one of the most delightful of all waterfalls in the dale: it is virtually hidden and can only be approached after a steep climb on foot. It can be viewed both from the

top and from below the falls. After heavy frost, spray from the waterfall freezes to create startling ice formations.

Goat Scar Lane links two moorland farms: Upper and Lower Winskill. Upper Winskill was the home of Tom Twistleton (1845–1917), one of the most prolific of the 19th-century Dales dialect poets, who modelled himself on Robert Burns, even sporting a plaid. His collection of poems 'Splinters Struck off Winskill Rock' (1867), includes his finest work. The path back to Langcliffe from here offers superb views down Ribblesdale from the top of Langcliffe Scar, with lynchets (ploughing terraces) very much in evidence.

Westwards from Little Stainforth the old packhorse way crosses a limestone ridge past Smearsett Scar to Feizor, the site of a monastic grange, and Smearsett and Pot Scar, both impressive craggy limestone escarpments. On the hillside to the south of the path is a stretch of drystone wall built with chunks of limestone, of massive proportion and primeval appearance, and reputed to be Celtic.

A footpath leads west from Stainforth across high ground to the hamlet of Feizor.

Helwith Bridge

NORTH OF HELWITH BRIDGE, the minor road leads up Ribblesdale along a shallow valley westwards to Austwick. Here, exposed from under the limestone surface, are ancient Silurian and Ordovician mudstones, siltstones and a form of hard gritstone known as greywacke. Coombes Quarry at Foredale, on the side of Moughton, has long been famous among geologists for the superb exposure of its contorted bands of ancient slates. Horizontal strata of limestone lie directly on top of the far older Silurian rocks, the intermediate beds of red Devonian sandstones being almost totally absent in the Yorkshire Dales because of the effects of erosion. In times past these quarries provided slate used by Dales people for a variety of purposes: roofing, cottage pavements, doorsteps, tombstones, gate-posts, porches, partitions in cow byres and even water cisterns.

Such hard rock also makes excellent road surface material, and given the closeness of the Settle-Carlisle railway and the demand for road metal, it is hardly surprising that large quarries have developed. Originally these used an extensive network of sidings and narrow gauge rope systems to link the quarries with the railway. The trackbed of the sidings remains, but the sidings themselves have long since been taken up and the quarries are now entirely served by road. Huge, mechanical diggers haul out the rock, which is crushed and transported by hundreds of heavy waggons along the busy B6479 between Horton, Helwith and Settle.

The Silurian quarries and the limestone quarries further to the north are now huge scars, bitten deep into the hillside on a scale which threatens even the vast Upper Ribblesdale landscape. Slim buttresses of unquarried slopes lie between the great craters, one of them at Foredale carrying a little line of quarrymen's cottages perched between the great faces.

Above the line of the quarries with all their noise and activity, is Moughton Nab. Moughton is a high limestone plateau, a fascinating area of scar, pavement and rare juniper trees, dating back to pre-glacial times. This is an area of Special Scientific Interest, close to the roar of industry, yet remaining relatively undisturbed.

A contrasting piece of nature conservation lies directly in front of the spoil tips of Dry Rigg Quarry at Swarth Moor, where low-lying peat bogs harbour a wide variety of orchids and other rare wild flowers, grasses and insect life.

Helwith Bridge has a comfortable and popular inn, used by walkers, potholers, quarrymen and local people alike. The Settle-Carlisle line follows the opposite bank of the river, having crossed two

Helwith Bridge does double duty as a river and rail crossing.

particularly impressive skew bridges across the Ribble at Sherwood. It was near Sherwood Brow, where river and railway share a narrow gorge, that the River Ribble was forced by railway engineers to change course, so that the railway could follow the old river bed on a more convenient line.

The Ribble Way follows a high-level path between Stainforth and Helwith Bridge to the east of the river, which climbs the steep hillside across rough pastureland above Bargh House Farm before joining the enclosed track which crosses from Sannat Hall Farm on the Littondale road, down to Helwith Bridge. A continuation of the path from Stainforth climbs up the shoulder of Pen-y-ghent to Churn Milk Hole – a small pothole – where it meets the Pennine Way.

The back road to Helwith from Little Stainforth climbs across the open expanse of Swarth Moor before joining the lane to Austwick, past the little hamlet of Wharfe with its Tudor houses. Wharfe Wood, to the south, is a beautiful deciduous wood on limestone, noted for the rare wild daphne which flowers there in February. A public path links Wharfe and Feizor, and high-level routes which lead back into Ribblesdale.

Horton in Ribblesdale

BETWEEN HELWITH BRIDGE and
Horton, railway and river share the
narrow valley floor, whilst the main
road takes a slightly steeper route into
the village.

Horton station, the first stop on the
Settle-Carlisle line beyond Settle, is a
popular starting point for walkers
enjoying a huge variety of routes in the
Three Peaks country and taking the
Pennine Way to Hawes or across the
fells into Littondale or Crummackdale.
The old Midland Railway station in
characteristic 'Derby Gothic' style, has
been carefully restored, much of the
work being done by volunteers; its
beautifully kept garden is worth a visit
in its own right.

Horton, a scattered village along the
main B6479 road, has two focal ponts:
the southern part, around the medieval
church, school and Golden Lion pub;
and the northern part, around the
station, quarry entrance and Crown Inn.
It is also a village with conflicting
interests. The huge ICI quarry and its

traffic dominates the town, and makes a
massive impact on the landscape, with
the quarry face running along the
western flank of the dale, and the
coppery-green settling ponds, machinery
and spoil tips. In common with other
quarry operators in the Dales, and in co-
operation with the National Park
authority, the company has made
attempts to screen the workings, with
grassy banks and tree planting.
Weekday lorry traffic is a nuisance in the
village; again, rail sidings which once
served the quarry have been removed.

*Horton in Ribblesdale, with the distinctive outline
of Pen-y-ghent (seen also above) in the background.
A public footpath is signposted to Pen-y-ghent
from the hamlet of Brackenbottom, east of Horton
Bridge.*

HORTON IN
RIBBLESDALE

Pennine Way
&
Ribble Way

P

R

B 6479

Ribble Way

However, many people in the village
find employment in the quarries, which
provide a valuable product for the
construction, steel and chemical
industries.

The other main interest here is
tourism. Being so very close to
Yorkshire's Three Peaks (see page 136),
the village is crowded at weekends with
parked cars and coaches. The pubs and
camp site are busy, as is the popular
Three Peaks Café and outdoor shop, a
haven for walkers and cavers. It is here
that Three Peaks walkers register for the
24-mile (38km) marathon which must be
completed inside 12 hours to receive the
appropriate rucksack badge. There is
also a local shop and post office, and a
regular bus service down the valley to
Settle.

Horton also lies on both the Pennine
Way and the Ribble Way, and a choice
of overnight accommodation for walkers
and backpackers is available in the
village. The Pennine Way northwards
from Horton to Hawes (see page 134)
via Cam Fell is a particularly fine 13-
mile (20.8km) ramble, and the
robustness of the broad tracks and green
lanes across well-drained limestone
ensures that no erosion problems
occur. The Ribble Way takes a more
meandering but also extremely
attractive route along the east side of the
valley to Ribblehead.

However, the village itself should not
be neglected. Particularly worth visiting
is the 800-year-old parish church of St
Oswald, dedicated to King Oswald of
Northumbria. It has a solidly built, 41-ft
(12m) high tower, dating from the late
14th or early 15th century and is
probably defensive in design, with
traces of older Norman work in its
fabric. The font, with its zig-zag
patterns, is also Norman, as are the piers
and arches of the nave. There is typically
Norman dog-tooth moulding on the
porch around the south door. One
specially fascinating feature is the
grooves caused by archers sharpening
their arrows on the side stones of the
door. It was common in medieval times
to carry out archery practice in village
churchyards.

Quiet lanes and field paths which
lead around the back of the village to
the east allow the visitor to quickly
escape from the weekend crowds in the
village centre. There is also a pleasant
riverside path carrying the Ribble Way
down the valley past Cragghill Farm
towards Helwith Bridge.

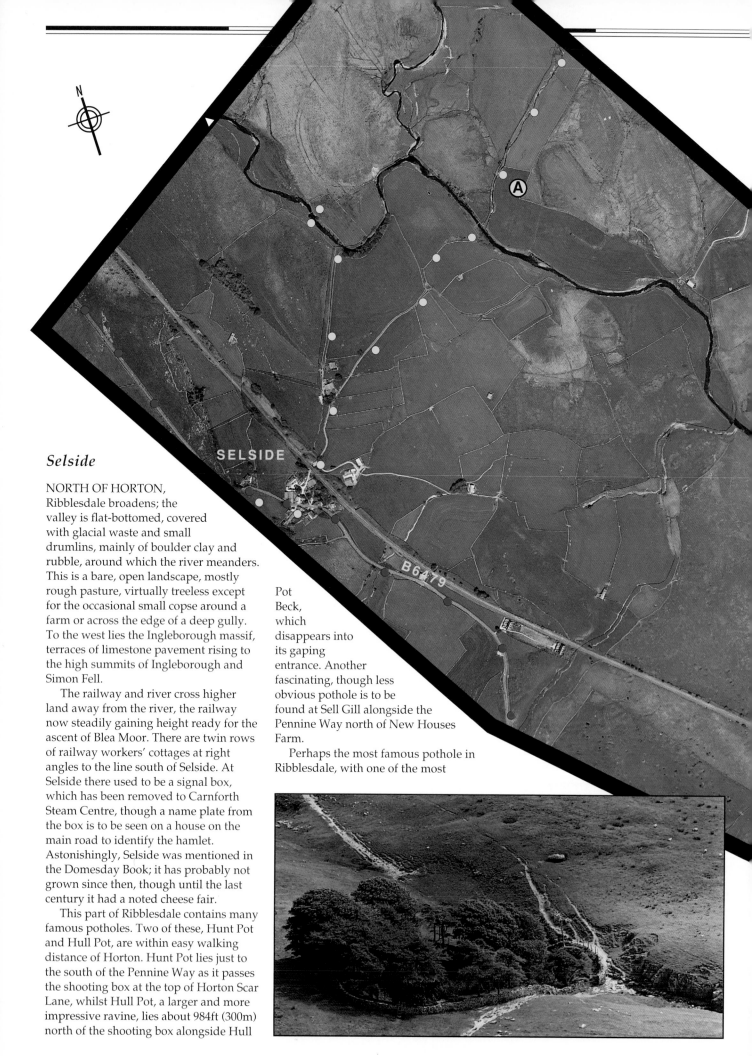

Selside

NORTH OF HORTON,
Ribblesdale broadens; the
valley is flat-bottomed, covered
with glacial waste and small
drumlins, mainly of boulder clay and
rubble, around which the river meanders.
This is a bare, open landscape, mostly
rough pasture, virtually treeless except
for the occasional small copse around a
farm or across the edge of a deep gully.
To the west lies the Ingleborough massif,
terraces of limestone pavement rising to
the high summits of Ingleborough and
Simon Fell.

The railway and river cross higher
land away from the river, the railway
now steadily gaining height ready for the
ascent of Blea Moor. There are twin rows
of railway workers' cottages at right
angles to the line south of Selside. At
Selside there used to be a signal box,
which has been removed to Carnforth
Steam Centre, though a name plate from
the box is to be seen on a house on the
main road to identify the hamlet.
Astonishingly, Selside was mentioned in
the Domesday Book; it has probably not
grown since then, though until the last
century it had a noted cheese fair.

This part of Ribblesdale contains many
famous potholes. Two of these, Hunt Pot
and Hull Pot, are within easy walking
distance of Horton. Hunt Pot lies just to
the south of the Pennine Way as it passes
the shooting box at the top of Horton Scar
Lane, whilst Hull Pot, a larger and more
impressive ravine, lies about 984ft (300m)
north of the shooting box alongside Hull

Pot
Beck,
which
disappears into
its gaping
entrance. Another
fascinating, though less
obvious pothole is to be
found at Sell Gill alongside the
Pennine Way north of New Houses
Farm.

Perhaps the most famous pothole in
Ribblesdale, with one of the most

spectacular entrances in Britain, lies on the other side of the valley on the hillside, about ½ mile (800m) west of Selside. This is Alum Pot, and it is easily reached along the enclosed track from Selside, going over a stile on the right where the track bears left. As this is private land, a small fee is payable at Selside Farm cottage in the centre of Selside for access to the Pot.

Alum Pot is an immense chasm, fenced and planted around with larches and pines, some 130ft (40m) across, 30ft (10m) wide and 200ft (65m) deep, from where it descends another 98ft (30m) or so into another undergound chamber, which is also fed by nearby Diccan Pot. A moorland stream flows into the chasm at its southern end, and when in spate produces massive amounts of spray as it cascades down the walls. It was this spray, lifted by currents of air, that caused early travellers to imagine that they were staring into the mouth of hell, and that what they were seeing was the smoke of hellfire. In winter the beck can become a sparkling sheet of ice. Ferns, small shrubs and lichen cling to the rock edge and into the cave. Alum Pot was first descended in 1847, by a group of cavers who approached the chasm from nearby Long Churn on precarious ropes. Nowadays cavers use ladders to go directly down.

Only a short distance along the path from Alum Pot is Long Churn, which, although it does not have such an impressive entrance, is relatively safe, and is often used by novice cavers. A number of fascinating features include the celebrated Cheese Press, a narrow gap for the slim to wriggle through on their stomachs, and Dr Bannister's Hand Basin, a pool and waterfall up which the energetic can easily scramble.

However, potholes are dangerous places prone to rapid flooding, and should only be tackled by the well-equipped under the direction of experienced leaders. It is also advisable to keep well away from the slippery entrance when peering into often highly dangerous shafts.

There are ample opportunities for ramblers around Selside, perhaps taking fell paths over Borrins and Sulber, then down Sulber Nick to Horton. Alternatively, it is possible to cross the footbridge over the Ribble by Hornsey Hill, east of Selside, (A) ascending Coppy Gill past Low Birkwith and High Birkwith farms. From there the route ascends to the Pennine Way, or follows linking paths over High Greenfield to Beckermonds in Wharfedale. The Ribble Way leads from Birkwith to Thorns Gill, and paths lead across God's Bridge – a natural bridge of solid limestone – via Ingmire Lodge to Ribblehead. A particularly interesting route southwards follows a high-level, panoramic path along a limestone pavement past Scale Pasture and Fawber to Sell Gill, returning down the Pennine Way track to Horton.

River Ribble

B 6479

The entrance to Alum Pot.

B6256

River Ribble

Ribblehead

Ribblehead

RIBBLEHEAD IS ONE of the bleakest, wildest places in the Yorkshire Dales, a vast hollow in the fells, with scarcely a tree to be seen, and little sign of human habitation. The fells, drained by little streams and side valleys that flow into the Ribble or the Doe, are the haunt of golden plovers and curlews, whose plaintive cries in the wind are a distinctive sound. It is an area of heavy rainfall: the rainclouds from the Irish Sea blow almost without impediment up the shallow valley between Ingleborough and Whernside, until they meet resistance at Cam Fell, and so empty themselves around Ribblehead, filling the streams until they are foaming torrents.

One immense, man-made feature dominates this valley – Ribblehead Viaduct. With its 24 tall arches, the highest of them 165ft (50m) above the ground, it was built mainly of limestone between 1870 and 1874, and required an army of navvies for its construction. The

2,629-yd (2,403m) long Blea Moor Tunnel lies 500ft (152m) under Blea Moor a mile (1.6km) to the north. Whilst the viaduct was under construction, the navvies lived in vast shanty towns on Batty Moss, part of the common, and it is still possible to see outlines of earthworks and narrow gauge tramways which carried materials for the works. At the peak of construction work, over 2,000 men lived here. The shanty towns had Biblical or Crimean War names – Jersualem, Jericho, Sebastapol, Inkerman, Belgravia – and a reputation for drunkenness, violence and disease. Salt Lake cottages, a rail workers' terrace about ½ mile (800m) south of Ribblehead, recall those days. The lineside quarry close by the cottages is now a National Nature Reserve protecting the orchids and twayblades that flourish there. Over 100 navvies, who died during the construction work on the railway, lie

buried in the tiny churchyard at Chapel-le-Dale, just off the Ingleton road. Many were the victims of disease exacerbated by appalling weather conditions. A plaque erected by the Midland Railway commemorates them.

Ribblehead Station survives, albeit with only the southbound platform, the northbound platform having been demolished in 1975 only weeks before the station reopened for special 'Dalesrail' ramblers' trains. Curiously, this station, which must be one of the remotest in England, serving only a couple of hamlets and a pub, has a commuter train: a daily service to Leeds starts at Ribblehead around 7am. The reason for this facility is that the morning commuter train serving

Settle has to travel to Ribblehead, where there is a signal box, before switching tracks to travel back into Leeds.

Ribblehead, well served by rail and with easy parking by the roadside verges, is a good point for an ascent of Whernside (see page 136). The Station Inn has a window in the rear of the bar with a view of the approach of the viaduct and a train seen approaching the viaduct is reputed to allow just sufficient time for an energetic rambler to sprint to the station in time to catch it.

Other less strenuous walks can be enjoyed from Ribblehead. One of the most delightful is to Thorns Gill, reached off the Ingleton road before Gearstones by a direct path. Here, there is a remarkable single arched packhorse bridge dating from the early 17th century, when it carried part of the Craven Way, an ancient packhorse road between Settle and Dent. It crosses a deep, limestone ravine where trout can usually be seen lazing in the peat-brown pools. Rowan trees and thorn bushes add to the special magic of this secret little valley carrying Gayle Beck, the main tributary source of the Ribble. A small cave, Catnot Hole, can be reached upstream from the bridge. Paths continue to the deserted hamlet of Thorns, only accessible on foot.

About ½ mile (800m) to the north is Gearstones, a ford where the Dales Way and the Roman road between Bainbridge and Ribchester cross from Cam End over Gayle Moor and into Dentdale. A footbridge avoids the ford. Here there was a celebrated drovers' inn and fair which, in the 18th century, attracted hundreds of Scottish drovers en route between southern Scotland and Malham. A market was held here every Wednesday until the 1870s. Gearstones remained an inn until the 1930s, and the building is now a farm and bunkhouse barn for walkers.

A branch of the Craven Way linked Hawes and Settle, and at Ling Gill on the Pennine Way, east of Ribblehead and accessible by fieldpath, there is an 18th-century bridge over Cam Beck, which crosses Ling Gill, a National Nature Reserve. This is a deep, glaciated ravine noted for its variety of wild flowers and shrubs. All are strictly protected. From Ling Gill the Pennine Way can be followed northwards over Dodd Fell to Hawes, or southwards past Old Ing to Horton.

N

B6479

Ribblesdale

Farming and Industry

FARMING PATTERNS IN the Dales go back to Anglian times. Around a typical Anglo-Saxon village, with its church and its 'headman's' hall, were common fields, which were rotated for arable crops, meadows and pasture, together with small enclosures for a few sheep and cattle. These were usually linked by a drove road, or 'outgang', and evidence of these can still sometimes be seen as a walled green way leading between fields to upland pastures. Later, 18th-century drystone wall enclosures often merely reflect these earlier field patterns. Often the arable fields utilised the well drained valley sides along which narrow ridged terraces, known as 'lynchets' or 'raines', were created, and whose outlines can still clearly be seen in soft winter or evening sunlight, or after light snowfall in areas such as Upper Wharfedale or Nidderdale.

The Norman Conquest imposed a powerful, feudal bureaucracy over the Dales, controlled by barons from great, heavily fortified castles at Skipton, Knaresborough, Richmond, Sedbergh, Bolton and Middleham. Vast areas of Wharfedale, Nidderdale, Wensleydale and most of Langstrothdale became

Above: Collecting hay in Coverdale.

Right: A Swaledale ewe.

protected 'forest', or hunting reserves, for the red deer and wild boar which were once common in the Dales. Fierce forest laws were imposed against any local peasantry found poaching.

But it was perhaps by granting vast acreages of their land to the newly established monastic communities of Benedictine and Cistercian monks, and Augustinian Canons that the Norman aristocracy had the greatest influence on Dales agriculture and industry. Much of the land given to religious houses was poor in quality and difficult to farm. So the monastic farmers began to specialise in the large scale production of the one product for which the climate and terrain was suitable – sheep wool. From a system of outlying granges the Cistercian monks of Fountains Abbey, for example, developed vast sheepwalks in Malhamdale which were linked by tracks to the abbey's other estates in Ribblesdale and in Borrowdale

in the Lake District. Vast surpluses of wool were produced which were gathered in the main grange at Kilnsey in Wharfedale, and then taken to the parent abbey at Fountains by packhorse to be stored in the great cellarium before onward carriage by packhorse and river boat down the Ure to York. From there it would be shipped along the Rivers Ouse and Humber, then

Left: A lead-ore crusher in Skipton's Craven Museum.

Below left: Muker Fair, Swaledale.

The monks were also among the first people after the Romans to exploit the mineral wealth of the Dales, particularly lead, and from medieval times until the end of the 19th century – when veins ran thin and foreign competition became overwhelming – lead mining was a major Dales industry. Fault lines between the limestone and gritstone areas of the Dales produced rich veins of galena - lead ore - in Nidderdale, Wharfedale, Malhamdale, Wensleydale and Swaledale. Whole communities grew up to provide manpower for the many lead mines and smelt mills.

At the same time, the Agrarian Revolution of the late 18th century resulted in widespread enclosure of much of the old common lands and on the higher open pastures, creating the rectangular, regular field patterns which owe more to the surveyor's rule than ancient field patterns. Enclosure increased the efficiency of farming but dispossessed the common people who owned no land. Ironically, many of these same people had to seek work erecting the miles of drystone wall that established the Enclosure and now make such a feature of the modern Dales landscape, crossing fells and moorland in gigantic lines.

The coming of the canals and railways and with them bulk supplies of cheap coal for steam power soon made water-powered textile mills in the higher dales uneconomic, and helped to concentrate manufacturing in the areas to the south of the Dales. But better communications helped to develop another, still important, Dales industry – stone quarrying. In the late 19th and early 20th centuries rail-served quarries and stone mines in Ribblesdale, Wensleydale and Wharfedale became major suppliers of limestone, sandstone and slates for the building, chemical, road and steel industries. Dairy farming was also given a boost as express trains took milk and cheese to cities as far away as London. These industries continue today even though road has largely replaced rail as a means of transport.

But the decline and eventual collapse of the lead-mining industry at the end of last century as seams dwindled and prices, through foreign competition, fell caused many thousands of Dales families to leave the area to seek work in the mills and factories of Lancashire or Teesside or across the Atlantic.

exported to the merchant princes of Florence.

By the 16th century Fountains Abbey was one of the richest monastic communities in the land. After the Dissolution the trade continued, with Dales wool being spun and woven by waterpowered mills in Dales villages - many of them established by monks but now in the hands of new private owners. Thus sheep farming, the backbone of Dales agriculture, and the foundation of the West Riding woollen industry, owes its origin to the monasteries of the Dales. The ancestors of the short-legged, hardy, black-faced Swaledale and Dales-bred sheep may have been first introduced by monastic farmers.

Dentdale

'A PICTURE OF terrestial paradise' – these were the words used by the experienced and unemotional agricultural surveyors, Messrs Rennie, Brown and Sherriff, when they came to Dentdale for the first time to prepare their report on the state of agriculture of the West Riding in 1793.

It is easy to see why the surveyors were so delighted by the dale. Facing westwards, it is, on the one hand, largely sheltered by the high fells from the cruel north and east winds. On the other, its western aspect brings more rainfall, creating lush pastures. The many little farms and small enclosures – hedges being as common in Dentdale as stone walls – also give a feeling of a well tended valley between the open moorlands. No doubt at that time the

Left: St Andrew's Church in Dent

Below: Dent station at the head of the dale.

Right: Dent, the only community of any size in the dale.

valley would seem even greener, as there were more farmers and farm workers available to prevent the higher upland pastures from being abandoned and turning brown with rushes and coarse grasses.

Dentdale is fortunate in being almost a cul-de-sac valley. The main road along the valley, especially beyond Dent, is extremely narrow – too narrow for large

waggons or coaches – and only negotiable by car with care. The top end of the valley has narrow bridges, tight curves and steep gradients that discourage casual traffic. Nobody simply drives through the dale on their hurried way to anywhere else – it's quicker to take an alternative route. Even though it's not all that far to the M6, and even though the large village

car park soon fills up in the summer months, this remains one of the quieter dales.

It's also one of the few dales to have its own railway station. Paradoxically, this is so far from the village it serves that quite a lot of people arriving at Dent station never get there, but disappear across the empty fells, heading for Ribblehead, Whernside or even Hawes.

Dentdale

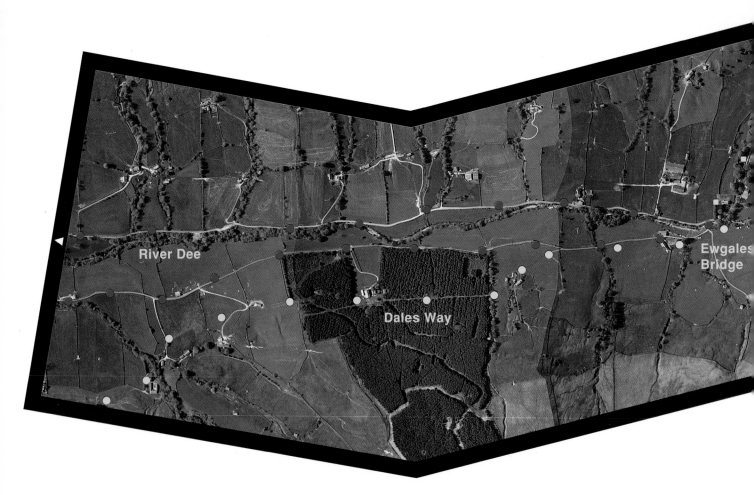

River Dee

Dales Way

Ewgales
Bridge

DENTDALE

Cowgill

THE RIVER DEE has its source high up on Wold Fell, above Newby Head, barely 200yds away from the streams which flow to form the infant River Ribble on Gayle Moor.

This bleak, central Dales watershed is crossed by the former Lancaster-Richmond turnpike road between Ingleton and Hawes. Near the summit, the minor road to Dent drops sharply into Dentdale, underneath the magnificent and much photographed Denthead Viaduct. The watershed is also crossed by the Dales Way footpath as it winds it way from Gayle Moor and Gearstones into Dentdale, following the narrow lane which runs alongside the river past Denthead youth hostel and the white-walled Sportsman Inn. The Settle-Carlisle railway runs underneath the watershed, through Blea Moor Tunnel. You can, in fact, trace the line of that tunnel over Blea Moor, along a public footpath which climbs from Little Dale, near the tunnel's southern entrance, and follows the line of huge brick ventilation shafts along the moortop before descending sharply,

through plantations, to emerge in the lane at Denthead.

There is no more spectacular way into Dentdale than by train. As you emerge from Blea Moor Tunnel on a speeding Sprinter train, a sudden burst of light greets you, followed by superb views of the green valley stretching out below. The line follows a long, narrow shelf engineered into the side of the fell. You cross the tall Arten Gill Viaduct, built out of black limestone over a deep gorge and moorland track. The viaduct stands on the site of the Dent marble works where, in the 1830s, a young Tynesider, William Armstrong, walking in Dentdale whilst on holiday with his wife, studied the 'inefficient' waterwheel driven by Arten Gill Beck and subsequently invented the world's first turbine.

At 1,150ft (350m), Dent has England's highest railway station. It lies at the edge of a deep cutting which, in severe winters, has been known to fill completely with snow. On one occasion a locomotive was trapped for several days, covered by drifts with only its funnel protruding. A snow fence made of rotting railway sleepers holds back the drifts. The station buildings are now a private house in the process of

restoration, but the waiting room on the southbound platform has been restored and reopened. The station master's house on the hillside just behind the station is reputedly the first house in England to be equipped with double glazing, because of its exposed position.

Dent station lies 4 miles (6km) from the village it serves, for most people the best part of two hours' walk away. But the magnificent views from the station platform down the whole of the Dale as far as the Howgill Fells (see page 150) are ample compensation. The steep, zig-zagging road into the valley floor forms part of a moorland pass which links Dentdale and Garsdale. It is known as the Coal Road because it once served high moorland pits, providing domestic coal for communities in both dales.

Lea Yeat, at the bottom of the steep hill from the station, once had a Quaker Meeting House, in what is now a private house by the roadside. There also used to be a shop, but nothing now remains except a telephone box and parish notice board. The Dales Way footpath follows a beautiful section of riverside from Lea Yeat Bridge, alongside a shallow gorge, the river running underground during periods of dry weather, leaving a rocky bed. Beyond Ewgales Bridge, where

there is a camp site, the path links scattered farms on the hillside and goes through a dense spruce plantation around a farm known as Little Town.

The back lane along the south side of Dale is scarcely wide enough to accommodate a car, with few passing places between the hedges, which in spring are creamy white with blackthorn and filled with wild flowers.

Cowgill, the hamlet lying at the side of the green tack which crosses the fells into Garsdale, has a little chapel dating only from the 1830s, built at a time when due to competition from the factories in the new industrial towns, the collapse of rural industries, especially hand knitting, was causing much hardship in the valley. In the 1860s the chapel was the subject of a remarkable controversy, having been registered in the name of Kirthwaite by the church authorities. This name was contested by Professor Adam Sedgwick, the great Cambridge geologist (1785–1873) who was born in Dent, and was a trustee of the chapel. In 1868, Professor Sedgwick wrote and published a pamphlet entitled *A Memorial by the Trustees of Cowgill Chapel*, including much local and natural history. By chance the pamphlet came into the hands of Queen Victoria, an old friend of Professor Sedgwick. The Queen ordered an Act of Parliament to change the chapel's name back to Cowgill. A subsequent 'supplement' to the memorial was published to celebrate the event and the two booklets now constitute a valuable record of life in Dentdale as it was when Adam Sedgwick grew up in the valley at the turn of the 19th century.

The highest station in England – Dent. Snow fences can be seen to the right of the track.

Dentdale

Dent

THIS VALLEY WAS largely settled by Vikings in the 10th century, and its settlements and field patterns still reflect their culture. Farms are typically long and narrow, and are situated either alongside a moorland beck or along the spring line, to take advantage of fresh water supplies. Each farm, which would have been occupied by a yeoman farmer or 'statesman' owning his own land, and not subservient to a feudal lord, has its share of good, rich, bottom meadowland, followed by hillside pasture and a section of high fellside in addition, perhaps, to areas of common land. Viking farms tended not to be grouped in small settlements which evolved into villages as were Anglian farms, but remained scattered, leaving Dent as the only centre of significance in the entire dale.

The valley didn't therefore have a Lord of the Manor as such, but did have 24 statesmen or sidesmen who determined the living of the parish, and usually ensured the parson and indeed the curate were local men. Adam Sedgwick was himself the parson's son, and several of his relatives were vicars of Dent.

Today public paths still link the old farms along the valley, farms such as Gibb's Chapel, where the 17th-century farmhouse still survives as a ruined barn. Gibb's Chapel was the setting for a once popular Victorian novel by Mary Howitt set in the dale – *Hope On Hope Ever*.

Two footbridges known as Nelly Bridge and Tommy Bridge link both sides of the river and the footpath between carries the Dales Way, then goes past an area of riverside caves and potholes through the limestone, including a deep pool known as Hell's Cauldron. Whernside Manor, built in 1790 in West Indian Plantation style, was the home of a slave trading family, the Sills, whose tragic history scholars suggest may have provided Emily Brontë with material for her novel *Wuthering Heights*. A former caving centre, it is now used for outdoor pursuits' training by army personnel.

To the south runs the tributary valley of Deepdale: it is as its name suggests, a deep, intimate dale of lush pastures and scattered farms. Tracks lead up to Whernside and Nun House Outrake on to the Occupation Road, a stony track which traversed the fellside below Great Coum.

Dent, with its narrow cobbled main street, is one of the finest of Dales villages – now an Outstanding Conservation Area. In former times many of the narrow, three-storeyed, white-walled cottages which line the main street had high balconies where Dent people would sit and knit. 'Knitting brass' being an important secondary source of income for dalesfolk when not tending their sheep or driving cattle, or sitting by the fire at night. So adept were Dent people at knitting socks, hats and gloves in great quantities for Kendal market, that they were dubbed by people who saw them at work as the 'Terrible Knitters of Dent' – 'terrible' in this case meaning ferociously fast. Dent-knitted socks kitted out the English army during the American War of Independence and against Napoleon. There was even a knitting school close to the village. Mechanised factories, and a decline in demand for men's long stockings as trousers replaced knee breeches in the 19th century, helped destroy the cottage industry and caused the town to suffer a long decline so by the mid-20th century it was less than a third of the size it had been at the end of the 18th century.

The old Church of St Andrew dates mainly from the 15th century but the

tower was replaced in the late 18th century. There are fine Jacobean box pews, and the chancel floor is paved with local Dent marble. There is a memorial to Professor Sedgwick in the church, and to other members of his family, including a second Adam Sedgwick, who was an eminent zoologist.

The little grammar school attended by Adam Sedgwick, where he was taught by his father, the parson, before going to continue his studies in Sedbergh School and then Cambridge, stills stands behind the church. In front of a cottage in the main street – now a photographic gallery – is a large pink Shap granite fountain, placed there by local people as a tribute not only to one of the great founding fathers of 19th-century geological science, but to a man who never forgot his native dale, and who remained a great local benefactor.

The village has a car park, camp sites, two pubs, cafés, a post office, an outdoor shop, and a choice of accommodation. It is a popular stopping place on the Dales Way, and in the summer months minibus services link it with Garsdale or Dent station, whilst school buses run down to Kendal.

Dent (formerly and more correctly Dent Town) is the only village in Dentdale. It is a charming place, with many of its streets cobbled from wall to wall.

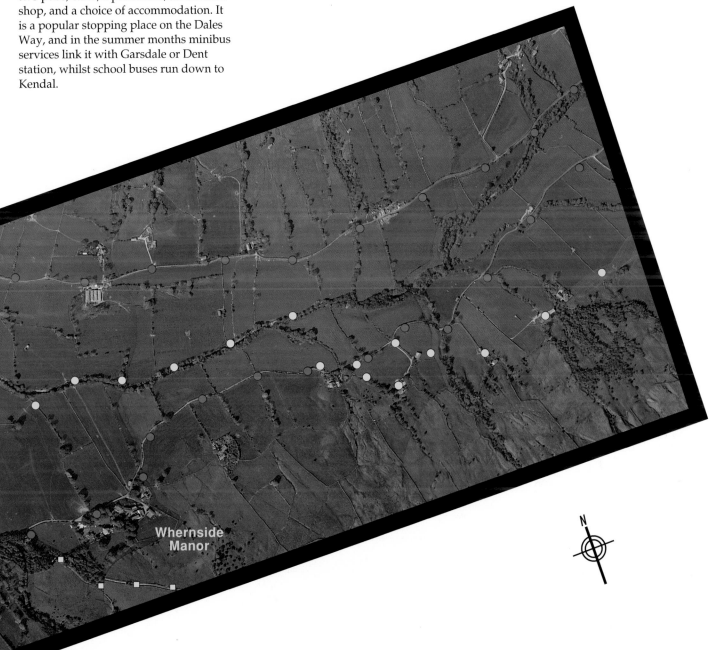

Whernside Manor

Dentdale

Gawthrop / Helmside

A REMARKABLE FEATURE of Dentdale is the number of old farms, many of them white walled, which date from the 17th and 18th centuries, and which have changed little over the centuries. Perhaps because this was never a prosperous dale, they were not rebuilt or expanded in late Victorian times, but remain as jewels of vernacular architecture. Sadly, only a minority are now working farms, with several used as weekend homes and holiday cottages. But the revival of new cottage industries, including weaving and craft centres, has helped maintain the population. High Hall, one such farm along a quiet lane to the south of the river, is now a Rare Breeds Centre, with unusual cattle and sheep. At Helmside, further down the river, is the Dent Craft Centre, occupying an old mill building and providing a retail outlet for many craft workshops in Dentdale and neighbouring valleys.

Gawthrop, one of the few hamlets of any size outside Dent itself, is a scatter of cottages and farms at the crossroads above the valley where the Barbondale road swoops down into Dentdale.

Barbondale is an intriguing valley, a narrow pass following a deep fold in the hills. It has been formed by the Pennine Fault, which separates the Carboniferous gritstones and limestones so typical of the Yorkshire Dales from the harder and older Silurian slates of the southern Lake District.

After a steep ascent from Dentdale, the road follows the bottom of Barkin Beck almost exactly along the fault line, with the steep fellside of Middleton Fell arising up to Calf Top. The contrast between the steep, almost geometrical slope to the north-west of the Barbon road, with outcrops of dark slaty rocks,

with the softer, more undulating countryside to the south could not be more marked.

Combe Scar, immediately above Gawthrop, is perhaps the finest example in the Dales of a cwm or corrie, a hollow on the hillside carved out by the action of glaciers, leaving a huge exposed scar of menacing, dark rock, the haunt of kestrels and other birds of prey which circle overhead. Keen ramblers can follow the public path from Barbon through the Barbon Estate and on to the edge of Middleton Fell, past Calf Top, Combe Scar and Holme Knott. The views of the Lakeland Fells and the Furness coast from the summit of Middleton Fell make this one of the finest fell walks in the Pennines. A less strenuous footpath goes from Gawthrop past Tofts and underneath Combe Scar.

The Pennine Fault crosses Dentdale

Continuing westwards, the River Dee meanders past Rotenbutts Wood on the left. The National Park boundary runs parallel to the dale from Gawthrop (further east) to Sedbergh.

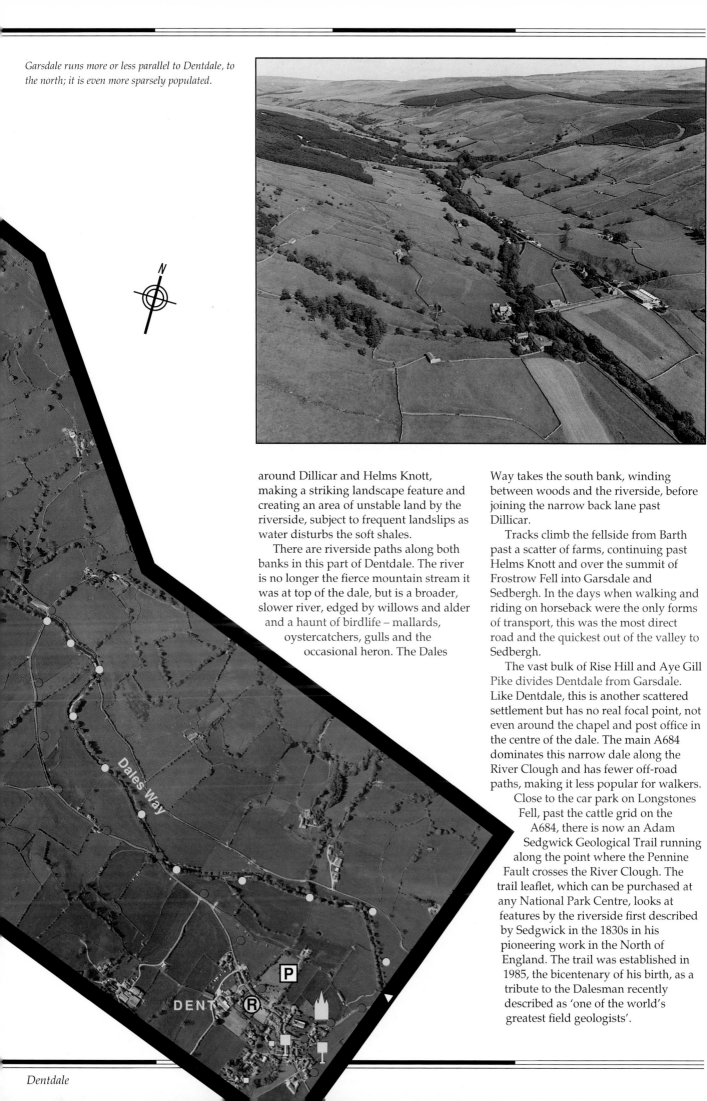

Garsdale runs more or less parallel to Dentdale, to the north; it is even more sparsely populated.

around Dillicar and Helms Knott, making a striking landscape feature and creating an area of unstable land by the riverside, subject to frequent landslips as water disturbs the soft shales.

There are riverside paths along both banks in this part of Dentdale. The river is no longer the fierce mountain stream it was at top of the dale, but is a broader, slower river, edged by willows and alder and a haunt of birdlife – mallards, oystercatchers, gulls and the occasional heron. The Dales Way takes the south bank, winding between woods and the riverside, before joining the narrow back lane past Dillicar.

Tracks climb the fellside from Barth past a scatter of farms, continuing past Helms Knott and over the summit of Frostrow Fell into Garsdale and Sedbergh. In the days when walking and riding on horseback were the only forms of transport, this was the most direct road and the quickest out of the valley to Sedbergh.

The vast bulk of Rise Hill and Aye Gill Pike divides Dentdale from Garsdale. Like Dentdale, this is another scattered settlement but has no real focal point, not even around the chapel and post office in the centre of the dale. The main A684 dominates this narrow dale along the River Clough and has fewer off-road paths, making it less popular for walkers.

Close to the car park on Longstones Fell, past the cattle grid on the A684, there is now an Adam Sedgwick Geological Trail running along the point where the Pennine Fault crosses the River Clough. The trail leaflet, which can be purchased at any National Park Centre, looks at features by the riverside first described by Sedgwick in the 1830s in his pioneering work in the North of England. The trail was established in 1985, the bicentenary of his birth, as a tribute to the Dalesman recently described as 'one of the world's greatest field geologists'.

Rash Bridge

AS THE RIVER DEE approaches its confluence with the Clough, the dale narrows between the vast grassy bulk of Holme Knott Fell to the south and Long Rigg to the north. The central part of the dale itself is blocked by a massive glacial moraine, through which the river cuts. The main road down the valley climbs steeply away from the river and over the shoulder of the moraine before descending to Millthrop Bridge and Sedbergh.

The pattern of scattered hillside farms continues right down the dale. To the south of the river, farms lie along the back lane, their architectural styles, thanks to use of the harder local slates, more akin to that of the Lake District than the Yorkshire Dales, with typical Lakeland slate chimneys.

Burton Hill Farm to the north of the river is an almost perfect late 17th-century farmhouse, nestling in a protected hollow in the hillside. A story relating to this farm in medieval times was that during a raid by the Scots a prized black mare was hidden in a stable constructed out of hay. Unfortunately the mare, hearing other horses, whinnied and gave herself away. The public path from the main road at Mire House goes past the farmyard, linking at Gate Manor with the top track to Sedbergh.

The Dales Way follows the lane along the south of the river as far as Rash Bridge. At Rash there is an 18th-century

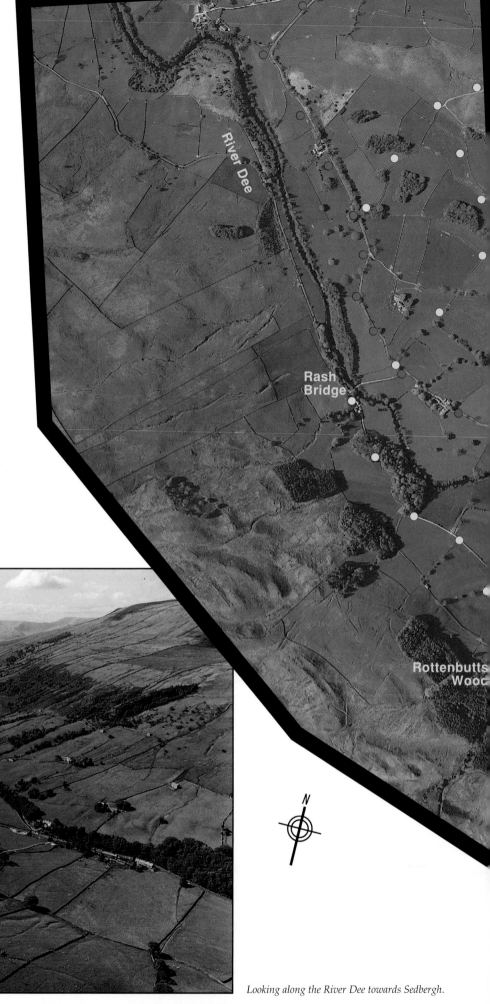

Looking along the River Dee towards Sedbergh.

watermill complete with its wheel which, partially restored by the boys of Sedbergh School, no longer functions. It was originally constructed as a corn mill, then converted to a carding and spinning mill, and finally became a joiner's shop.

The Dales Way crosses Rash Mill to the main road, before ascending to the old enclosed green way which crosses the edge of the Long Rigg Fell past the golf course. From the top of this track, where it crosses the open fell, there are superb views across to Sedbergh, with its magnificent green backcloth of the Howgill Fells, before the track descends into Millthrop.

Alternative routes lead around the base of Holme Knott past Holme and Catholes Farm, where there is a camping barn for walkers, into Sedbergh, an area of fragile beauty, with woods, fields and a narrow, wooded river gorge. Sadly, this area, known as Elysian Fields, is now threatened by a new golf course scheme complete with large car park and clubhouse.

At Abbot Holme there is a picturesque, narrow hump-backed bridge across the River Dee. Just to the north of this bridge the Rivers Dee and Rawthey meet, at a point best observed from the Dales Way footpath

The roads through Dentdale and Garsdale meet at Sedbergh.

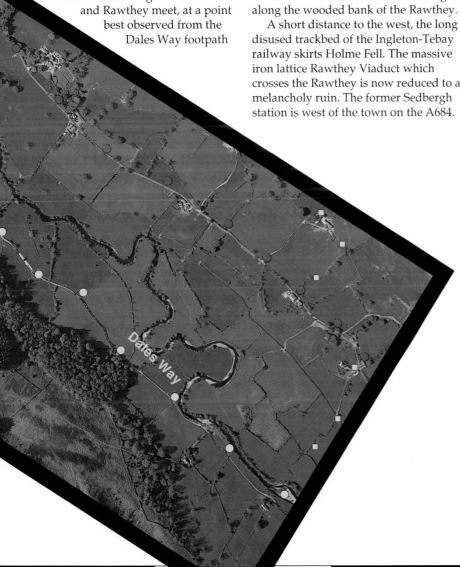

to the north as it travels from Sedbergh along the wooded bank of the Rawthey.

A short distance to the west, the long disused trackbed of the Ingleton-Tebay railway skirts Holme Fell. The massive iron lattice Rawthey Viaduct which crosses the Rawthey is now reduced to a melancholy ruin. The former Sedbergh station is west of the town on the A684.

From Abbot Holme, paths and the narrow lane westwards lead to Holme, where there is an ancient ford across the Rawthey, almost certainly dating back to Roman times. The bridleway continues to Middleton Bridge and the confluence of the Rawthey and the Lune, where the high-level path from Middleton Fell and Holme Knott descends past Fellside Farm to Jordan Lane.

Millthrop, immediately south of Sedbergh is, as its name implies, an old mill village, where there was formerly a riverside cottonmill. In later years yarn used in carpet manufacture in the West Riding was woven here. There are attractive stone-built mill cottages along Millthrop's narrow street. Millthrop Bridge across the River Rawthey, a good salmon and trout river, is a deep buttressed stone bridge dating from the early 18th century and still carrying the main road into Dentdale.

Dentdale

Sedbergh

THE OLD GREY STONE town of Sedbergh is the largest settlement within the Yorkshire Dales National Park. It is a fascinating town to explore in its own right, as well as an excellent centre from which to discover the Cumbrian part of the Yorkshire Dales, including the Howgill Fells (see page 150). It enjoys a superb, sheltered position to the south of the Howgills with two peaks, Winder and Crook, overlooking the town.

Sedbergh's name derives from Old Norse meaning 'flat topped hill'. This might relate to Castlehaw, the Norman motte and bailey castle whose foundations can still be observed as twin, flat-topped grassy mounds along Castlehaw Lane at the back of the town. No doubt it was because of Sedbergh's strategic position, guarding the entrances to both Garsdale and the Upper Rawthey valley, that the castle was constructed, but it seemed to decline in importance in later years and fell into ruin. Between the 12th century and 1974 Sedbergh was part of the old West Riding of Yorkshire, and though it is officially now in Cumbria, there is still a strong feeling among many local inhabitants that its roots lie in Yorkshire.

The oldest part of the town is around Main Street, a narrow, winding street whose cobbles have recently been restored. Several of the shops go back to the early part of the 17th century, and a notable feature of those on the south side are the long through-yards which extend behind the street, some with their workshops still standing. One of them, Weavers' Yard, behind Webster's chemist shop, was where the first weaving looms were established in Sedbergh. At the rear of the chemist's shop is a fine, broad 17th-century chimney. In parallel Railton Yard a wooden outside spinning gallery can be seen. These were once common features in this part of the Dales and Cumbria, being a place where women would spin wool, taking advantage of the available daylight, whilst being sheltered from the weather.

There is a small Wednesday market in the Joss Lane car park which which goes back to the town's market charter of 1251. An 18th-century shop on the main road by the car park is now the National Park centre.

The parish church is Norman in origin, and contains almost every style of ecclesiastical architecture from that period until the present. There are memorials to Sir John Otway, a Royalist and local landowner, and of John Dawson, the 18th-century Garsdale shepherd, doctor and mathematican, a largely self-taught mathematical genius who taught Adam Sedgwick and many of the country's leading mathematicians.

It was beneath a yew tree in the churchyard that, in 1652, George Fox preached one of his most powerful

Sedbergh with the Rawthey valley beyond. The southern part of the town is dominated by the buildings and playing fields of the famous public school.

Winder

A683

Ⓐ

sermons before going on to establish the Society of Friends, or Quakers.

About a mile (1.6km) west of the town, and linked to Sedbergh by footpath (A) past Birks Mill, is Brigflatts, one of the most famous and beautiful early Quaker meeting houses in Britain, dating from 1675. When it was first built the Friends were too poor to put in a ceiling and lined the roof with moss. It has an extended wooden gallery and a peaceful garden.

Sedbergh town is dominated by its famous public school with its teaching buildings, residential accommodation, chapel and playing fields. It was founded in 1525 as a chantry school to benefit poor boys in the area. Most of the school dates from the late 19th and early 20th century, but the oldest surviving part is the neo-classical building on Dent Road, dating from 1716, which now houses the library and a small museum. Evans House, north-west of the church, was built in the 1750s as the school house. Adam Sedgwick was only one of many noted scholars educated here; another famous scientist was George Peacock (1791–1858), one of the greatest astronomers of his day. Hartley Coleridge, the poet son of Samuel Taylor Coleridge, was a master there for a time, until sacked for frequent drunkenness.

Though most of the original water-powered textile mills which provided industry in Sedbergh have found other uses, including a chicken farm, Fairfield Mill has survived. Set on the A684 Gardale road just east of the town, this Victorian mill has machinery dating from the 1930s, and Pennine Tweeds produce traditional fabrics here.

Shops, pubs, cafés and accommodation are available at Sedbergh. There is a good choice of walks from the town. Paths lead directly on to the Howgill Fells (B), whilst the riverside path, know as the Rawthey Way, follows the river from Buck Bank in the east to beyond Brigflatts. The Dales Way takes the Rawthey Way westwards, crossing the main A683, past Ingmire Park, the former home of the Otways which was destroyed in a disastrous fire, to High Oaks, a lovely Jacobean farm, and up the River Lune. At Killington Bridge a small riverside Access Area lies alongside deep, slaty pools by the River Lune – a favourite picnic and bathing area.

Dentdale

Eden valley

is almost certainly derived from the Saxon, meaning 'the river through the woods'. Much of this 35-mile (56km) long river flows through the red sandstone country of East Cumbria, between the Lake District and the North Pennines. From its source high in the Yorkshire Dales on Black Moor Fell above Aisgill, the river passes through some of the most dramatic countryside in the North of England, across the Stainmoor Gap and along the foothills of the North Pennines to the Solway coast.

The Settle-Carlisle railway, with stations at Garsdale and Kirkby station, provides the ideal high-level way of seeing the upper part of this valley. The B6259, between the Moorcock Inn and Kirkby, is also scenically impressive, whilst walkers have a choice of high- and low-level routes, including part of the Settle-Carlisle Way, which follows the railway line, and the Eden Way, a 77-mile (123km) footpath which runs from Black Moor to Rockcliffe Marsh, where the Eden joins the Solway near Carlisle.

Left: Lammerside Castle to Birkett Common.

Above: The remnants of Lammerside Castle.

Right: Hell Gill, right on the National Park boundary.

ONE OF THE remarkable engineering feats of the Settle-Carlisle railway is its exploitation of Dales topography, curving along the sides of valleys and, wherever possible, using the lie of the land to avoid expensive tunnels and viaducts.

From Dentdale the line goes through a relatively short tunnel, under Rise Hill, to emerge at Garsdale Head. Here it follows the valley side high above the road before bearing northwards to the top end of Wensleydale. At Aisgill, the summit of the line, it crosses the watershed into Mallerstang, in the Upper Eden Valley, before following the River Eden all the way into Carlisle.

'Eden' is an appropriate name for this most beautiful of Cumbrian valleys. Its name owes nothing to Adam and Eve; it

EDEN VALLEY
Garsdale Head / Lunds

GARSDALE HEAD, on the A684 between Sedbergh and Hawes, was once an important railway junction, where the much missed Wensleydale line from Northallerton, Leyburn and Hawes met the Settle-Carlisle line. The trackbed of the branch to Hawes, closed in 1959, is still a distinctive feature, a smooth strip of green swinging away eastwards through the heather. A signal box and sidings remain. The station, with its two waiting rooms, has recently been restored since its reopening for regular passenger trains in 1985. Moorland streams now provide the water supply for steam locomotives hauling the Cumbria Mountain Express and other Steam Specials. These stop at Garsdale station for water and a photo opportunity, bringing hundreds of enthusiasts on to the lineside to photograph the gleaming engine.

Garsdale station was, for many years, known as Hawes Junction. There were fine canopies over the station platforms, an engine shed, water troughs fed by a water tank (below which there was a village reading and meeting room) to allow Scottish Expresses to fill their tenders at speed, and a turntable. It was here that, in the early years of the century, a locomotive was being turned

Moorcock Inn on the A684, which runs right across the Yorkshire Dales.

when a fierce gust of wind began to rotate the engine. No amount of effort could stop the rotation until, after an urgent telegraph down to Settle, someone hit on the idea of pouring sand into the turntable pit. This eventually acted as a brake and forced the train and turntable to grind to a halt.

The hamlet of railwaymen's cottages which grew around the station now consists largely of holiday homes, but new life has returned to the station with a regular train service, this being a popular park-and-ride station for Hawes people going to Leeds or Carlisle. It is also a starting point for some of the most thrilling walks in the northern Dales, particularly in the direction of Kirkby Stephen. Minibus services link Hawes and, in the summer months, Swaledale and Sedbergh.

Paths from the station lead into Garsdale, over Rise Hill into Dentdale, and across into Grisdale. This cul-de-sac valley of scattered farms is known as 'The dale that Died', following a Yorkshire Television programme which recorded the decline of communities in the little Dale.

Beyond Moorcock Inn the B6259 joins the railway line; they continue in close consort along the Eden valley.

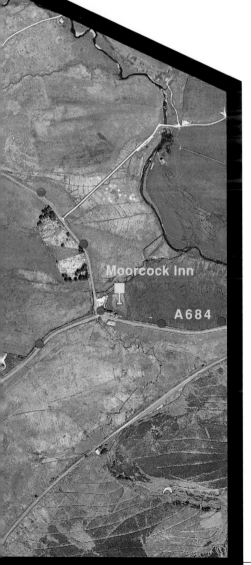

Keen ramblers have a choice of routes up Baugh Fell, a broad, boggy hill capped by cairns, into Uldale, an almost deserted valley leading to the Howgills. There are also walks up Swarth Fell and on to Wild Boar Fell, one of the finest and grandest ridge walks in the Pennines.

East of Garsdale, the Settle-Carlisle line curves over the A684 across the fine Dandry Mire Viaduct. The tiny Methodist chapel which once served this isolated community still stands, though dwarfed by the viaduct.

The Moorcock Inn, at the crossroads of the A684 and B6259 Kirkby road, was once known as the Guide Post Inn. Sheep fairs took place here, and a small show and sheep sale is still held in September in fields behind the inn.

Until 1826, when the present road to Kirkby was built, the main route between Hawes and Kirkby Stephen was an ancient green road which runs above Cotter End, known as the High Way. Probably dating from the Bronze Age, this route was used for travellers both on horseback and by coach. It was also an important route for packhorse trains, and for drovers. Its most famous regular traveller, however, was Lady Anne Clifford, who travelled by coach between

her castles in the mid 17th-century, with her full retinue behind her. Several now deserted farms, including, at High Dyke, a former packhorse and drovers' inn, lie along the route.

The hamlet of Lunds, a focal point for a number of scattered farms on the shoulders of High Abbotside, has a tiny early 18th-century church with a little bell-cote, reached by track (A) and bridge over the infant River Ure. One of the smallest churches in the North of England, and probably built by local people, it is now disused and semi-derelict, the tombstones in its little graveyard leaning or fallen into open pasture. A Corpse Way led to Lunds via High Dyke from Cotterdale, and was reputedly used by the people of Cotterdale to reach the nearest consecrated ground. The footpath can still be followed across the fell.

Paths lead from the church up to Shaws, a romantic, rocky gill with a waterfall. The wooden pavilion close by was, during the 1920s and '30s, the home of Scott Mackfie, an authority on gypsy folklore. Mackfie built the road and planted the trees along the drive. His home later became a youth hostel which closed in 1985 – a matter of weeks before the reopening of Garsdale station.

Eden valley

Aisgill Cottages / Hell Gill

THE RIVER URE has its source at Ure Head on a fell known simpy as Sails, 2,186ft (666m) up on a high lonely ridge of Abbotside Common. Barely 330yds away from the stream, already known as the River Ure as it bustles down the hillside, is a tributary stream of the Eden. Rain falling in the Ure will emerge in the North Sea at the Humber estuary: that tributary flows into the Solway and Irish Sea below Carlisle. This is truly the watershed of England.

The valley, shared by river, road and railway, has a desolate beauty. As you look north the distinctive, flat-topped Wild Boar Fell dominates the landscape. A fell path crosses from Grisdale over White Birks Common to join the bridleway (A) along the western side of the valley, and soon becomes a green way, slightly elevated.

An old farm by the roadside, Shaw Paddock, was, during the last century, an inn known as Shaw Paddock Inn and for a time in the 1820s, the Bull. It was popular with drovers bringing their cattle down from Scotland to one of the great Northern or Midland cattle fairs in days before the railways. Apparently it was not uncommon to see a drover playing the bagpipes as he marched with his herd: this supposedly encouraged the weary cattle on their journey.

Shaw Paddock lies on a junction with a bridlepath which climbs up past limestone outcrops to join the High Way, following the moor edge from Cotter End at Hell Gill.

Hell Gill is a deep, rocky gorge in the underlying limestone, through which flows Hell Gill Beck, the stream which drains from Black Fell Moss and forms the Eden. At one time this stream, known as Red Gill at its source, flowed southwards into the Ure, but glacial drift at the end of the last Ice Age blocked its flow, forcing it to turn northwards to join other streams forming the Eden, and thus allowing it to be claimed by Cumbria.

Hell Gill now forms the county boundary between North Yorkshire and Cumbria, and for bureaucratic rather than geographic reasons, marks the northern boundary of the Yorkshire Dales National Park, though the Upper Eden through Mallerstang has some of the most dramatic and awe-inspiring scenery of the Northern Dales.

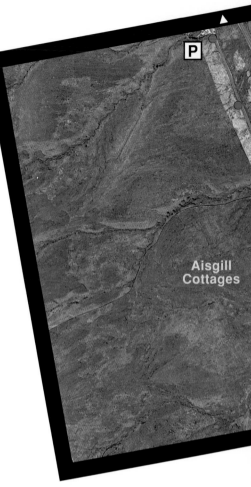

Wild Boar Fell rises up to the north-west of Aisgill Cottages. It falls just outside the National Park.

The old bridge which carries the High Way across Hell Gill probably dates from the early 18th century. There are remarkable views down into the 60-ft (18m) deep rocky gorge from the bridge parapet. Legend has it that Dick Turpin made an amazing escape higher up the gill by leaping across on Black Bess, where none dared follow after him. It is more likely to have been the 18th-century Westmorland highwayman, Will Nevison, who was active in this area; he was known to be a frequent visitor to High Dyke Inn above Lunds.

So busy was the High Way in times past that local farmers' wives would set up stalls on or near the bridge selling nuts, cakes and herb beer to passing travellers. North of the bridge it becomes a superb green way, curving

Hell Gill
Bridge

River Eden

Settle & Carlisle Way

(A)

River Ure

B6259

along the shoulder of the fellside below
Mallerstang Edge before gradually
losing height down towards The
Thrang, en route for Pendragon, Kirkby
Stephen and Brough.

The track downstream from Hell Gill
Bridge, past Hell Gill Farm, descends to
Aisgill Cottages, passing a small
waterfall on the right – Hell Gill Force –
which is particularly impressive after
heavy rain.

A signboard by the side of the
railway line at Aisgill announces the
fact that this is the highest point on the
Settle-Carlisle line. It is also the highest
point on any railway in England, being
1,169ft (356m) above sea level; the only
main line in Britain which exceeds it is
the Perth-Inverness line in Scotland.
The bridge on the main road just above
Aisgill is a popular point for railway
photographers, as the gentle curve of
the line gives a fine profile of steam
engines as they approach the summit
from the north, with Wild Boar Fell in
the background.

A small nature reserve by Aisgill
Cottages lies alongside a welcoming
café and craft centre, strategically
placed as a midpoint on low-level
walking routes between Garsdale and
Kirkby Stephen.

Eden valley

Mallerstang

MALLERSTANG, AS THE Upper Eden valley is known, is a glacial valley, carved out and deepened by ice. The steep-sided, U-shaped valley is flanked to the west by the massive summit of Wild Boar Fell and to the east by Mallerstang Edge, Hugh Seat and High Seat.

This is a dale of isolated stone farms which seem, when set against the vastness of the fells, to have grown out of the very rock of which they are made.

The Settle-Carlisle line, having passed its summit, now begins the long and gradual descent of the Eden valley. The railway is built on a carefully engineered shelf along the steep slopes of Wild Boar Fell, much of it in cuttings, increasingly elevated above the valley bottom. The intertwined river and road drop steeply towards Kirkby Stephen until the railway once again appears high up on the fellside.

Wild Boar Fell reputedly earned its name when the last wild boar in England was killed here. The discovery of a wild boar's tusk in the 15th-century tomb of Sir Richard Musgrave during the Victorian restoration of Kirkby Stephen church gives some credence to the legend.

The mountain rises 2,324ft (708m) above sea level; a trig station stands on the flat summit, which forms a high, gritstone-capped plateau ending at The Nab, a line of crags and a superb

viewpoint looking down into the great chasm of Mallerstang. In fine weather the view extends as far north as Cross Fell, the highest peak in the Pennines, and Criffel, in southern Scotland; it also takes in the Solway Firth, the Howgill and Lakeland peaks to the west and the rounded summits of the Dales to the south and east.

Wild Boar Fell forms the highest of a

long line of fells, mainly open, unfenced common, acid peat, rough grazing and heather. These have grown over sandstones and shales, which are themselves set on a vast Carboniferous limestone base. The whole massif forms a gigantic ridge, terminating in a dark cliff face above Mallerstang but sloping away at gentler gradients westwards towards the Howgill Fells. Swarth Fell, Wild Boar Fell, Little Fell and Greenlow Rigg are a great quartet of linked summits which provide a magnificent high-level ridge walk from Garsdale, ending at Wharton Common and Birkett Fell south of Kirby Stephen.

An alternative route from the Mallerstang valley to the summit of Wild Boar Fell follows the bridlepath from Hazelgill farm, about 3 miles (4.8km) north of Aisgill Cottages. The route crosses over the northern slope of Wild Boar Fell by High Dolphinsty, from where a path leads to the summit. The bridleway then continues across to the hamlet of Stennerskeugh, its name indicating its Viking origin, to Ravenstonedale. Stennerskeugh Clouds is a magnificent area of limestone pavement.

Aisgill, the stream which gives its name to Aisgill summit, has its source on the southern slopes of Wild Boar Fell, and flows through two small ravines, White Kirk and Low White Kirk, before going under a viaduct on the railway line to join the Eden by Aisgill farm.

Equally splendid for keen fell-walkers is the great ridge to the east of Mallerstang: Mallerstang Edge itself and

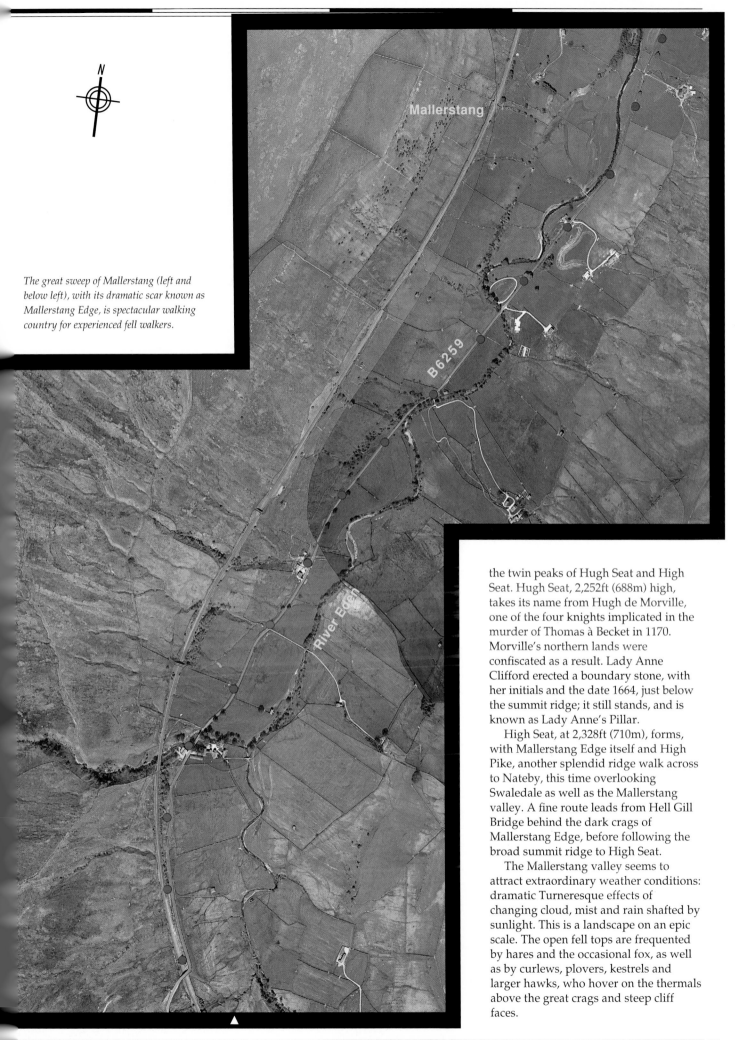

The great sweep of Mallerstang (left and below left), with its dramatic scar known as Mallerstang Edge, is spectacular walking country for experienced fell walkers.

the twin peaks of Hugh Seat and High Seat. Hugh Seat, 2,252ft (688m) high, takes its name from Hugh de Morville, one of the four knights implicated in the murder of Thomas à Becket in 1170. Morville's northern lands were confiscated as a result. Lady Anne Clifford erected a boundary stone, with her initials and the date 1664, just below the summit ridge; it still stands, and is known as Lady Anne's Pillar.

High Seat, at 2,328ft (710m), forms, with Mallerstang Edge itself and High Pike, another splendid ridge walk across to Nateby, this time overlooking Swaledale as well as the Mallerstang valley. A fine route leads from Hell Gill Bridge behind the dark crags of Mallerstang Edge, before following the broad summit ridge to High Seat.

The Mallerstang valley seems to attract extraordinary weather conditions: dramatic Turneresque effects of changing cloud, mist and rain shafted by sunlight. This is a landscape on an epic scale. The open fell tops are frequented by hares and the occasional fox, as well as by curlews, plovers, kestrels and larger hawks, who hover on the thermals above the great crags and steep cliff faces.

Eden valley

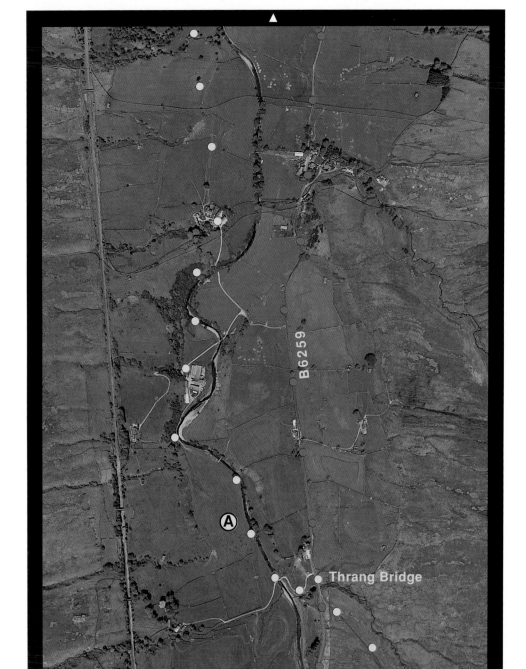

B6259

Thrang Bridge

River Eden

Settle & Carlisle Way

Ⓐ

Thrang Bridge

THE HIGH WAY probably crossed the River Eden at Thrang Bridge and followed what is now the Eden Way (A) along the west bank of the river past Shoregill Farm and Sandpot to Pendragon Castle. Quiet riverside paths can now be followed here between farms and scattered barns.

Being so close to the Stainmore Pass through the Pennines, this valley was extremely vulnerable to Scottish raids in the 14th century. This may partially explain why, to this day, it has no larger settlements than Outhgill.

Outhgill is a particularly interesting hamlet. The little Chapel of St Mary, first built in 1311, was rebuilt by Lady Anne Clifford when she was restoring her hereditary castles. She travelled this way in 1663, at the age of 74, coming from Skipton over the Stake Pass, then following the High Way from Hawes across Hell Gill and staying at Pendragon Castle whilst various 'improvements' to her properties were being undertaken. Lady Anne, Dowager Countess of Dorset, Pembroke and Montgomery and Sheriffess of Westmorland (1590—1676), was the last of the Cliffords of Skipton and Appleby, and had to wait 43 years after the death of her father to inherit her ancestral estates. A woman of immense personal courage and energy, she had a reputation for generosity, helping the old and the poor, endowing almshouses and using her wealth for the good of the community.

James Faraday was the village

blacksmith in Outhgill during the early part of the 18th century. His son, Michael Faraday, became a world-famous scientist, one of the discoverers of electricity. The Faradays belonged to a Nonconformist sect known as the Sandemanians, a breakaway group from the Church of Scotland, who had much in common with the Inghamites, followers of Benjamin Ingham, a notable preacher in the north and Scotland.

A replica of the famous Eden valley Jew Stone now stands in a small enclosure in the hamlet. This 7ft (2m) high piece of Dent marble (black limestone) is inscribed in Latin and Greek, as well as with mystic symbols and the Star of David. The post recalls William Mounsey's long walk in 1850 along the River Eden from Rockcliffe Marsh to its source on Black Fell Moss above Hell Gill, along a route almost identical with what is now the Eden Way. William Mounsey (1808–1877), known as the Jew of Carlisle, was not, in fact, Jewish, despite his deep sympathy with the Jewish religion. A prosperous solicitor and a member of a wealthy Cumbrian family, he wore a beard and dressed in the contemporary Jewish fashion. He was also interested in the occult, and spent a good deal of his spare time walking around Westmorland, carving mysterious heads and epigrams in the soft red sandstone of the Eden valley.

Originally, the pillar was erected high on Black Fell Moss close to the source of the Eden, the termination of Mounsey's walk. Unfortunately the remarkable

memorial was smashed by navvies working on the Settle-Carlisle railway during the 1870s, and proved impossible to repair. But thanks to the efforts of local people, and an appeal which received help from people in both England and Israel, a replica Jew Stone has been erected on Outhgill as a memorial to Mounsey.

It is said that most of the drystone walls surrounding farms on the valley floor in Mallerstang were built by lead-miners from Keld in Swaledale in the late 18th century, who found that they could supplement their income by contract-walling.

Winters in Mallerstang are notoriously fierce. Snow ploughs from Carlisle often have to work hard to keep the railway line open. In 1947, hay had to be brought into the valley by special train, the roads all being closed, and tipped over the embankment into adjacent fields to be delivered to farms by sledge. In the long and fierce winter of 1963, the road up to Outhgill was blocked and had to be opened by the Highway Department ten times. In some places cuttings had to be dug through snowdrifts that were up to 25ft (7m) deep.

Ing Hill House, now a hotel, was originally a Georgian farmhouse, believed to be on the site of a hunting lodge in the ancient Forest of Mallerstang, which extended into the valley from Stainmore.

Outhgill village, with Little Fell in the background.

Pendragon Castle / Birkett Common

ACCORDING TO LEGEND, Pendragon Castle, standing on a low mound immediately above the east bank of the Eden, was the birthplace of Ughtred or Uther Pendragon, father of King Arthur. Despite Uther's alleged magic powers, he was unable to alter the course of the River Eden to provide the castle with a defensive moat. As an old rhyme expresses it:

Let Uther Pendragon do what he can,
The Eden will run where the Eden ran

Whether there was ever any genuine Arthurian connection is doubtful, but the castle site of Pendragon does date from the 6th century when Romano-British tribes were trying to organise some form of defensive action against Saxon invaders. The present stone-built castle, which almost certainly replaced an earlier timber and earth fortification, dates from Norman times. In the 12th century, it was owned by the ill-fated Sir Hugh de Morville (see page 97); an old tale recalls Morville having a vision of the murdered archbishop from the castle window, in an outline along the profile of the hillside which it is claimed can still be seen today.

De Morville's estates were confiscated by Henry II as punishment for Becket's murder, but they were restored by King John to his nephew, Robert de Veteripont. In due course they were inherited by Isabella de Clifford, remaining in the possession of the Cliffords for many generations. A former King of Scotland, Edward Balliol, was entertained here in 1337 but Pendragon was later destroyed and sacked by the Scots. After, further rebuilding and destruction some years later it was finally restored by Lady Anne Clifford in 1660. She gave her ancestral castle stables, a brew house, a coach house and a wash house, and built the bridge over the Eden close by, turning it all into a more civilised dwelling. It was unfortunately dismantled by the Earl of Thanet, a descendant of Lady Anne in later years, and in 1773 there was a further major collapse of masonry. Nevertheless, the castle remains an evocative ruin and a link with Mallerstang.

A narrow lane – Tommy Road – crosses Wharton Fell from Pendragon to the main Sedbergh road, crossing an area

The ruins of Pendragon Castle. Formerly a Clifford ancestral home, it finally collapsed in the late 18th century after being dismantled some years before – by a Clifford.

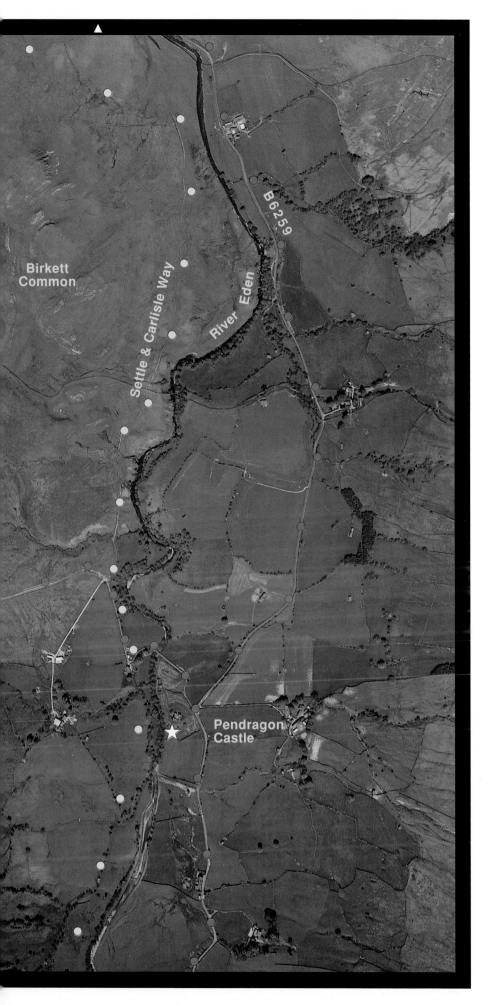

of wide open, unfenced common. Fell
ponies, brown and piebald, can be seen
wandering here, grazing on the open
land. They are not 'wild', however: every
autumn the ponies are rounded up and
herded to Water Yat Bottom near Birkett
Common, where pony sales take place.

The underlying limestone forms
outcrops at several points in this area,
particularly around Birkett Common;
here, until late in the last century, several
small field limekilns were used to
produce hydrated lime for agriculture.
Birkett Common is a particularly
fascinating, spiky green hill. An old track
curves around its northern slope, and it
lies close to an open area of meandering
riverside, popular with both ponies and
picnickers.

This is an area of increasingly complex
geology, of shake holes and spring lines
in the limestone, and of light green
limestone scenery, with its sweet
pastureland. To the north, in the Nateby
area, a long, narrow rib of New Red
Sandstone, so typical of the Eden valley,
meets and for a time blends with the
older Carboniferous limestones,
sandstones and shales of the Dales. The
railway engineers had a difficult job
building the Settle-Carlisle line in this
area, including Birkett Tunnel, owing to
the unstable nature of the rock near
major geological fault lines. Even to the
present day, landslip is likely to occur
after melting snows or heavy rain.

Lammerside Castle, just to the north of
Birkett Common, originally dates from
the 12th century, but was rebuilt and
strengthened in the 14th century as a pele
tower, for protection against the Scots.
Though only a small ruin isolated in a
field (a public bridleway goes close by),
its 6-ft (1.8m) thick walls and massive
barrel vaulted stone roof above the
surviving ground floor of the keep are
still impressive. Much of it is now
crumbling and the building is in a
dangerous state. Lammerside was the
home of the de Quertons, later known as
the Whartons, before they moved to the
grander surroundings of Wharton Hall,
close by. According to legend, an
underground passage is supposed to
have connected Lammerside and
Pendragon Castles.

Eden valley

Lammerside / Nateby

IN ORDER TO MAINTAIN its
continuous gradient as it makes it way
from Aisgill summit to Smardale, the
Settle-Carlisle railway avoids Kirkby
Stephen, keeping to the high land above
and to the west of the town. Kirkby
Stephen West station, as it was originally
known, is therefore a considerable
distance away from the town it is
supposed to serve, up a long, winding
hill along the main A685 Tebay road.
Nevertheless, the railway remains an
important lifeline for this otherwise
isolated community, with young people
using the early morning train every day
to go to college in Carlisle.

Ironically, the station which lay much
closer to the town, closed in 1959, this
was Kirkby Stephen East on the
Stainmore Line from Darlington and
Barnard Castle to Tebay and Penrith.
Even higher in altitude than the Settle-
Carlisle line, the much lamented trans-
Pennine route was built to carry Durham
coke to the Cumberland steelworks, but
as this trade declined there was
insufficient passenger revenue to sustain
maintenance costs. As recently as the
1950s, this was the main route for
summer specials from Tyneside and
Teesside to Blackpool and the Fylde
coast. Holidaymakers now go by coach
and car along the A685.

Walkers use Kirkby Stephen station as
a valuable transport link to or from the
northern edge of Mallerstang and Wild
Boar Fell. Paths lead via Wharton Dikes
and Bull Gill across to Wild Boar Fell and
Birkett Common, crossing expanses of
open country, with few other people to
disturb the larks, kestrels or
sparrowhawks.

Wharton Hall, lying on a small
eminence just above a curve in the Eden,
is one of the finest fortified house in the
North. It dates from the 14th century,
and has been given many extensions over
the years. A great hall and kitchen was
added by Thomas, 1st Lord Wharton in
1540, and a grand gatehouse was built in
1559. A tablet over the courtyard
archway, also dated 1559, has the
Wharton family's coat of arms and motto,
'Pleasur in acts darmys'. The building,

B6270

Wharton Hall, along with Pendragon and Lammerside Castles, testify that this was former border country that needed defending against the Scots.

partially built in warm Eden valley red sandstone, has surviving fortifications and narrow, pointed mullioned windows. It is a private house and part of a busy and very modern working farm.

The Whartons first made their name in the 1540s, when the same Thomas Wharton who built the hall and kitchen fought and routed a large army of Scots invaders at Solway Moss. Despite having a smaller force he took 1,500 prisoners. Three years later he helped to attack and destroy Dumfries. In return for these exploits, he was created Baron Wharton in 1544. His son Thomas kept up the military tradition, but his grandson make the mistake of entertaining James I at Wharton in 1617, resulting in deep debts. The 4th Baron, Phillip, 'Good Lord Wharton', was a Presbyterian who supported the Parliamentarians in the Civil War, but became a Royalist after Cromwell declared himself Lord Protector. He is perhaps the best-remembered Wharton because of the Wharton Bibles, given to children who had learned seven psalms by heart. The Whartons were active in the development of Swaledale lead-mining, and one of the family wrote the words to what became one of the most subversive songs in the country – 'Lillibullero'.

On Gallows Hill, above Wharton Hall, near the railway, is an ancient earthwork,

a remarkable example of ancient strip fields or lynchets, especially noticeable after light snow or in early evening sunlight.

Nateby is a small, compact village around the crossroads with the Swaledale road, with a shop and an inn, the Black Bull. Geologically, the area is especially fascinating: sandstone and limestone meet here, and a concrete-like conglomerate known as brockram or breccia is formed, outcropping around the back of the village and in the Eden. It is much used for building in the area. A narrow, enclosed bridleway leads from Nateby into Kirkby Stephen, and the B6265 climbs steeply eastwards over Tailbrigg and Lamps Moss into Swaledale.

To the north of this road is a high fell topped by a series of nine tall, ancient cairns – Nine Standards Rigg. The origin of these mysterious cairns is unclear; they were probably boundary stones, but the old legend is that they were erected by English defenders of Mallerstang in the 14th century. Flags – 'standards' – were raised on their tops in order to fool invading Scottish armies into believing that a mighty army lay in waiting beyond the brow of the hill. The Coast to Coast footpath now winds its way past the Rigg on its way from Kirkby Stephen into Swaledale.

Eden valley

Kirkby Stephen

THE OLD MARKET TOWN of Kirkby Stephen lies where ancient roads from Brough and the Stainmore Pass cross the Eden, before branching towards Tebay and up Mallerstang. It has probably been a place of trade and worship for well over a thousand years. In the parish church there lies a remarkable 8th-century Anglo-Danish 'Loki' stone, one of only two such examples known in Europe, depicting the Scandinavian devil held in chains, presumably to control his evil powers. St Stephen's Church dates from 1220 but almost certainly occupies a far older site, and is built of warm red sandstone. Like a small cathedral, it has a long, elegant nave, 13th-century arcades and a sturdy 16th-century tower. Grand tombs with effigies of the Musgraves and the Whartons date from the 15th and 16th centuries. At 8 o'clock every evening a curfew is still sounded by the ancient Taggy Bell, once regarded by local children as a demon.

The old buttermarket is an impressive colonnade forming the entrance to the churchyard. Erected in 1810 with money left by John Waller, a prosperous naval purser, as a shelter for both churchgoers and traders, it emphasises the importance of Kirkby Stephen as a market and trading centre. Until the last century, when tithes were abolished, the local people paid their tithes in cash on the Trupp Stone, an old gravestone, in the churchyard.

The market square, outside the churchyard, has hosted regular markets since 1351; at one time there were six annual fairs. There is still a Monday market and regular animal auctions. Until 1814 the square was also used for bull-baiting.

Because of Kirkby Stephen's strategic position as a halfway point on roads across the Pennines, there were at one time no fewer than 17 public houses and inns here, catering for stagecoach travellers as well as market traders. Most have long vanished, but a good choice of inns and cafés remain to cater for the needs of modern Trans-Pennine travellers, including Coast to Coast walkers. The youth hostel, in a former chapel, replaces an earlier hostel in the Friends' Meeting House which was one of the oldest in the British Isles.

Kirkby Stephen is a curiously elongated town, over a mile (1.6km) in length, an example of the ribbon development of the 18th and 19th centuries. Shops and houses stretch down the long main street and along the main roads which fork to the south of the town. This means that the riverside is always close by, with several quiet alleyways and snickets leading via Frank's Bridge, an ancient stone footbridge, to riverside meadows and woodland. There is a small disused weir here, with quiet riverside alders, and among the birdlife to be seen are mallards, martins, swallows, herons and the occasional kingfisher. Further upstream, the path through the woods goes past some fascinating formations, formed from breccia, on the riverside.

Back lanes on the opposite side of the town lead out along Croglam Lane to Croglam Earthwork, a small prehistoric

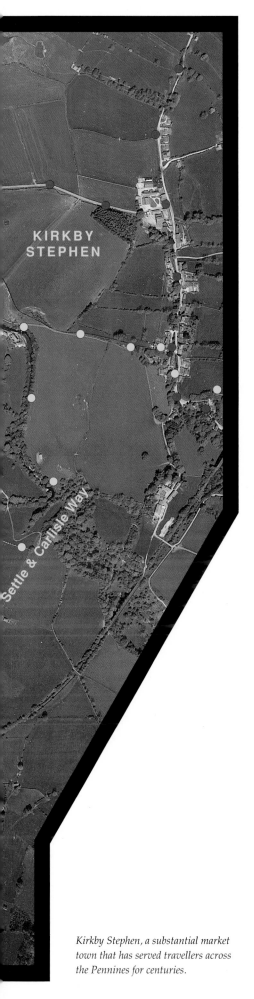

Kirkby Stephen, a substantial market town that has served travellers across the Pennines for centuries.

fort, probably of Iron Age origin. An ancient enclosure around the castle may have been used as a cattle shelter during Danish raids in the 8th and 9th centuries.

The village of Hartley lies to the east of Kirkby Stephen, and is reached by fieldpath or lane along an old Corpse Road; the bridge across the river is still known as Coffin Bridge. For many years, Hartley was dominated by Hartley Castle, built in the 13th century as the seat of Sir Andrew de Harcala, a soldier during the reign of Edward II who was made Earl of Carlisle in recognition of his services to the crown. His inability to halt the advances of Robert the Bruce and willingness to compromise with the Scots led to his execution for treason in 1322. His castle was occupied until the 18th century by the neighouring Musgraves, who then demolished it and used some of the stones to extend their own manor house at Edenhall, near Penrith.

Hartley lies close to an interesting area of limestone outcropping, much of it forming impressive scars and crags, partially wooded. There is also a large limestone quarry, developed after World War I, which until recently was serviced by a remaining branch on the Stainmore railway, between the quarry and the Settle-Carlisle line at Appleby.

There are also archaeological remains to be seen here, including early bellpits from which copper and lead ores were mined. A smelt mill came into operation as lead-mining expanded in the 18th century, and numerous small field limekilns can still be observed in the area. Mining finished in 1884, but tailings or waste tips continued to be worked for years afterwards.

Eden valley

Swaledale

SWALEDALE IS, for many people, the finest of all the Yorkshire Dales: an intimate, winding valley along the River Swale from Richmond to its headwaters on Birkdale Common.

Curiously perhaps for such a lovely valley, the Swale can be one of the most ferocious and destructive rivers in England, a fast flowing, and for the most part a benign and picturesque stream but which after sudden storms or melting snows on the high fells can rise with frightening speed and sweep away all before it, frequently demolishing yards of drystone wall, tossing boulders like corks,

destroying footbridges and undercutting embankments.

Like Wensleydale, Swaledale has earned the epithet Herriot Country, mainly because so many films have used the dale as a romantic backcloth to the tales of the North Country vet and his occasionally awkward clients. Tourism, particularly in the larger villages, has increased noticeably as a result.

But this is a valley which, by its scale and nature, only reveals its real beauty to the walker, and a dense network of footpaths awaits the keen rambler, linking villages and climbing into steep side

valleys, crossing fellsides. The Pennine Way makes its way across the top of the valley by Kisdon, but perhaps even more ramblers have in recent years enjoyed Alfred Wainwright's 190-mile (304km) Coast to Coast footpath which, since its television coverage, has become one of the most popular of all long-distance trails. The Coast to Coast path crosses the Dales from east to west between St Bees Head on the Irish Sea Coast and Robin Hood's Bay on the North Sea, and takes in the whole of Swaledale along the north of the valley from Nine Standards Rigg to Richmond and Easby Abbey.

Left: Swinner Gill joining the dale east of Keld. There is a good view of the gill from the Pennine Way on the other side of the river.

Right: Looking eastwards along the dale past Grinton. Richmond is some 10 miles (16km) beyond the village.

Below: One of the handsomest towns in the Dales, Richmond is a fascinating place to explore on foot. Its castle can be seen on the north bank of the river.

SWALEDALE

Richmond

RICHMOND, LIKE SKIPTON, owes its existence to a mighty medieval castle, built in 1070 by a Norman warlord, Alan Rufus, son of a Breton count who was granted the fee of Richmondshire soon after the Conquest. It was situated close enough to the ancient Saxon regional settlement of Gilling to the north to keep potentially rebellious Saxons in order. A huge, impregnable south-facing cliff overlooking the River Swale was chosen for the stronghold, whilst the mighty keep, some 108ft (32m) high, was added in 1146 by Earl Conan.

It remains an impressive fortress, with walls, towers and dungeons being used as a military base over the centuries. Three kings, two of Scotland – William the Lion and David II – and one of England – Charles I – were imprisoned here at various times. Now looked after by English Heritage, it is open to the public most days of the year. The view from the top of the keep across the rooftops of the old town and into the market place with its tall obelisk is said to be one of the finest from any building in the North of England, York Minster not excepted.

Richmond's raison d'être, *its castle, still dominates every part of the town which grew up below it.*

There are walks not only round the walls themselves, but along the Castle Walk below, with views along the wooded riverside and downstream across the rapids at the base of the castle rock.

An old legend tells of King Arthur and his knights sleeping in a hidden cave under the castle awaiting a call to save England. Accidentally discovered by a local simpleton, Potter Thompson, who was unable to blow the horn to awaken them, they sleep on for eternity.

Richmond began life as a garrison town, and remains one to this day, the garrison now being at Catterick Camp, an important army headquarters some 2 miles (3.2km) to the south-east. The former Trinity Chapel in the market place is the Green Howards Museum, with relics and a history of one of the country's leading regiments.

The town which grew up clustered around the rear of the castle was protected by a wall, fragments of which still survive. Permission to build the wall was granted to the free burghers of the town by Edward II in 1315 to help protect the town against Scottish invaders. At the Bar, just along from the market square, is the only survivor of the five original gateways. Many of the narrow lanes and alleyways which lead off the busy market place have evocative names such as Frenchgate, Friar's Wynd, Bargate and Pottergate – where Frances l'Anson lived in the 18th century, better known as The Lass of Richmond Hill in the folk song.

Franciscan friars settled in the town in 1258 but nothing remains of their friary except the beautiful 15th-century

Greyfrairs Tower near the town centre. What has survived is the remarkable Royal Georgian Theatre, opened in 1788, which, because it was used as a warehouse for very many years, escaped alteration and is now Britain's finest preserved theatre of the period, containing the oldest painted stage scenery in the country. There are many fine Georgian houses and streets in the town, whilst in the field off Cravengate is the Culloden Tower, a neo-Gothic structure built on to the base of an ancient pele tower to commemorate the defeat of the Jacobites in 1746.

The Richmondshire Museum in Ryders Wynd tells something of the long story of Richmondshire from the founding of the castle in 1070 to the present day. It includes the set for James Herriot's surgery from the first BBC television series.

Richmond is now an important regional shopping and administrative centre, and the headquarters of the District of Richmondshire, which roughly covers the ancient Saxon wapentake. Buses link the

town with Darlington Station (its railway was an early Beeching victim) and with Upper Swaledale and Wensleydale, making the town a good centre from which explore the northern Dales.

Upstream from Richmond Bridge, the dale is thickly wooded, especially along its southern steep-sided flank, through Billy Bank Wood and Calf Hall Woods. Known collectively as Hudswell Woods, they are both National Trust properties, noted for bluebells in spring. There is a choice of riverside and woodland paths and attractive circular walks, and a picnic site can be found at Round Howe, close to the footbridge across the river from the car park. Paths climb up to Hudswell village with its old church and pub. The views back from the higher paths across the Dale and to Richmond are particularly impressive, and include the famous view of the town painted by Turner.

Another popular, level walk from Richmond Castle leads downriver past the old railway station on the opposite bank – a preserved building now a garden centre – to Easby Abbey, a small Premonstratensian abbey and a particularly evocative ruin. The gatehouse, built in 1300, is virtually intact.

Whitcliffe Woods / Marske

WHITCLIFFE SCAR FORMS the cliff edge of a high terrace along the north side of Swaledale, below which the dale carves its way, with the river and main road following the winding valley floor.

Just off the back lane between Richmond and Marske, north of the river, in a field marked by two stones, is Willance's Leap, commemorating the amazing (accidental) leap across the Scar made by Robert Willance and his mare in November 1606. Robert Willance, a prosperous and adventurous lead-miner from

Richmond, was out hunting with a group of friends but they were separated and Willance got lost in dense fog. Unaware of where he was, he galloped towards the cliff edge, realising too late to hold the animal back, and horse and rider plunged down 200ft (60m). The mare was killed outright, but Willance, clinging on to her back, survived with a broken leg, which later had to be amputated. According to tradition the leg was buried under a stone in Richmond churchyard. Willance lived to become an Alderman of Richmond, and after his death in 1615, according to slightly macabre local humour, 'he was laid beside his leg'.

Stones were placed by Willance at the point where the horse took the fatal leap and although the view from the top of the Scar along the dale is spectacular it is most certainly not a place to leap across on horseback. From the top of Beacon Hill, just to the north of Whitcliffe Scar, it is possible to see the towers of York Minster on a clear day. Whitcliffe Woods, close by, are noted for the variety of their shrubs, trees and wildflowers, and for butterflies in the summer months. Hag Wood, to the south of the river, is another fine National Trust woodland. There is a busy camp and caravan site on the river close by.

Marske enjoys a lovely, sunlit setting above the deep wooded valley of the Swale. Its sturdy little church, though modernised, dates from the 12th century; the bridge across Marske Beck has arches from the 15th. There are clusters of grey cottages and a handsome 18th-century hall

A path from Richmond leads through Whitcliffe Wood and along Whitcliffe Scar. This is a view back towards Richmond.

set in parkland. This was for many years the home of one of Swaledale's most distinguished families, the Huttons. Matthew Hutton became Archbishop of York between 1595 and 1606, only to be outdone by a later Matthew Hutton, who became Archbishop of York and later Archbishop of Canterbury in 1757. A 60-ft (18m) high obelisk on the hillside above the road to Reeth was erected in 1814 to yet another Matthew Hutton as a memorial, and was placed at one of his favourite viewpoints across the dale.

The limestone valley carrying the little Marske Beck down the hillside into the Swale is curiously wide. This is because it was the overflow channel of the great Stainmoor glacier which covered the area to the north, its meltwaters, carrying abrasive silts, forcing their way down into the Swale and carving out this side valley. At Clints, just above Marske, there was a smeltmill to which, in the 18th century, lead ore was brought from Arkengarthdale for smelting.

The moorland road from Marske northwards follows a serpentine route over Gayle Moor and Holgate Moor past an area known as New Forest. This was an area which in late Anglo-Saxon times was notorious for wolves, but by the 12th century the wolf already faced extinction, and Earl Conan of Richmond, when granting the monks of Jervaulx pasturage in the New Forest, stipulated that no hounds or mastiffs were to be taken there so that the wolves would not be driven from the pastures. Perhaps the reason was to preserve sport, but it is nonetheless perhaps one of the earliest examples in the Dales of an attempt at species conservation.

There are remains of extensive lead-mining in these moors, with deep shafts; and there are other problems besides. Warning notices along many points of these moorlands advise visitors to keep to main tracks and paths. Much of the area has been used for military training, including firing ranges, and unexploded shells remain a hazard. There are many isolated and deserted hamlets and farms in this area, where there was once considerable farming and industrial activity.

Applegarth, the hamlet below Whitcliffe Scar, once formed part of the hunting grounds belonging to the Fitzhughs of Ravensworth. It is worth taking the minor road from above Whitcliffe Scar and travelling across High Moor to Kirkby Hill, with its isolated hilltop church, then continuing down to Ravensworth where, close to the village with its large green, are the massive ruins of Ravensworth Castle. This was the former stronghold of the Fitzhughs, powerful barons in Plantagenet times, who were authorised by Richard II to extend their castle and park. The Fitzhughs were once wealthy and influential landowners in the area, owning huge estates, but by the 16th century there were no more heirs; the vast estates were divided between relatives and the mighty castle was left to go to ruin.

Hartley Park

SOUTH-WEST OF MARRICK, road and river twist south and west down a valley which steepens and narrows. The main A6108 leaves Swaledale and, climbing out of the valley, heads due south across Downholme Moor for Downholme, Bellerby and Leyburn.

Downholme was once a much larger community than at present, when local lead and coal mines provided a living for a larger population. Its church was formerly owned by Coverham Abbey and though it has largely been rebuilt, there are some interesting headstones in the graveyard. The inn, the Bolton Arms, indicates the village's links with the Scrope family of Bolton Castle when it formed part of one of their deer parks. The foundations of the old manor house can just be seen close to the village.

Wolburn Hall, about 1½ miles (2km) along the main road to the south, is a superb example of a fortified manor house, largely Elizabethan in date but with many earlier features. There is a cobbled courtyard surrounded by defensive crenellated walls, and the remains of a chapel. A room with a bay window overlooking the road is known,

for reasons that are obscure, as Mary Queen of Scots' room. The house was restored by the Huttons of Marske in 1882, and is now privately owned.

The main road down Swaledale, the B6270, forks right and descends to the riverside through the woods of Hartley Park, where a tight curve takes it over the little wooded valley of Gill Beck.

Visible from the road across the river, to the east of Marrick, is the surviving tower of the Priory of St Mary, a house of Cistercian nuns. Not much is known about this small community as it was sacked by the Scots in 1342, who also carried off several of its charters. According to one story, a member of a local family called Ellerton always accompanied the prioress on her journeys from the convent, took messages for her or provided a horse, and gave her and the convent hospitality once a year. The convent was valued as having an annual income of only £15 10s 6d (about £15.51) at the Dissolution in 1536, not a great sum even allowing for the vast difference in currency values compared with the present day. It was surrendered 'without murmur or grief' by Johanna, the last prioress. Tombstones of two of the prioresses, Petronella, who died in

1251, and Ellen, who died in 1268, are preserved inside the ruined walls of the nave.

The 'grey old village' of Marrick lies on a hillside around 1,000ft (304m) above sea level, high above the main valley, surrounded by scattered farms and commanding extensive views. A moorland track leads across to Hurst, an isolated hamlet with little else but an inn and a former mine agent's house lying in desolate moorland, a full 1,250ft (380m) above sea level. In former times the village was known as Red Hurst and its inhabitants as 'Redshanks' because of a rust-red iron (chalybeate) spring in the village.

The road from Marrick crosses a landscape scarred and pockmarked

River Swale

B6270

with lead-mine workings, deep shafts, washing floors and hundreds of spoil heaps. This was ancient and rich lead-mining territory, well worked and reworked. According to some authorities it contains some of the oldest mine workings in the Dales. Many of the workings go down to a great depth, indicating ever more desperate attempts to trace new veins of ore. A pig, or long bar, of lead with the name 'Adrian' inscribed on it was discovered in some old workings last century and taken to the British Museum (from where it has long since vanished) and indicates that the mines were being worked in the time of Emperor Hadrian, in the 2nd century. One theory was that the mines lay close to a Roman penal settlement, where felons were sent for crime or misdemeanour into a harsh and punishing climate.

Close by the crossroads above Marrick, along a little walled lane, are the ruins of Marrick smeltmill, one of the largest in the Dales. Lead left here by cart and packpony for sale at Richmond market was eventually transferred to Stockton, then shipped to London. One reason for the building of the railway between Darlington and Richmond in the 1840s was to reduce the cost of transporting the lead and bring in cheaper coal from the Durham coalfield for smelting. There were plans later in the century to extend the railway further into Swaledale, perhaps as far as Reeth, but by that time the veins were becoming exhausted and prices had fallen.

All that remains of the 13th-century Priory of St Mary, at Ellerton, near Marrick.

Marrick / Fremington / Grinton

A LINE OF OVER 300 steps, known as the Nuns' Causey, leads down from Marrick village to Marrick Priory, a small Benedictine nunnery by the Swale. The nunnery was founded by Robert de Aske some time between 1154 and 1158. Although it was endowed with seemingly adequate land for income, so poor were the sisters by the mid-13th century that in 1252 visitors at the nunnery guest house were requested to stay one night only. At the Dissolution in 1539 only 12 nuns were still there. A famous painting by Turner, using more than a little artistic licence, shows the nunnery and its tower as an Italianate ruin standing high above the roaring gorge of the Swale. In fact, a few ruins, a farmhouse and a church tower are all that remain. The ruins have been turned into a comfortable outdoor and field study centre belonging to the Diocese of Ripon, where young people can stay to explore the northern Dales. There is accommodation for up to 30 people. The Coast to Coast footpath passes the nunnery on its route between Reeth and Richmond.

Riverside paths lead (32km) from Marrick Priory along the Swale to Grinton, an Anglian settlement clustered around the ancient bridge over the Swale. It is also the site of the oldest church of the dale, part of a huge parish extending over 20 miles (32km) in length along the whole dale – hence its impressive proportions for what would otherwise be a small community. The old church probably occupies an early Christian, perhaps even a pagan site. In fact it is an amazing patchwork of architectural styles and periods, with fragments of the early Norman church, a 12th-century tower arch, a 15th-century arcade, and a 16th-century chapel and tower. The whole edifice was fully restored in 1896.

One curiosity is the grave, in the aisle, of Ann Barker, who died in 1652 and who, contrary to the law of the time (designed to help the wool trade), was buried in

linen. Her father was fined £5 – a substantial sum – for this 'offence', which thankfully was the last such case recorded in Britain. Because for many centuries Grinton was the only consecrated ground in the dale, corpses had to be carried long distances to be buried, over fellsides and along the riverside, in specially constructed baskets carried on shoulder slings by the bearers. Surviving portions of the ancient Swaledale Corpse Way can still be traced in the Upper Dale.

This is an area rich in archaeological remains. Cutting its way high across the dale, below the grey limestone scar of Fremington Edge (between Fremington and Grinton), is a series of dykes, rampart and ditch structures which were almost certainly Iron Age defensive fortifications, possibly forming a boundary between rival tribal settlements. A large earthwork by the riverside at Grinton may have been linked to these defences.

Fremington is another small Anglian settlement. Not far away, at Fremington Hagg, a substantial hoard of Roman military equipment, including silver harnesses, was discovered in the 1830s. It

FREMINGTON

GRINTON

River Swale

B6270

Cogden Hall

N

Grinton Lodge now makes a fine youth hostel; it also has field study facilities.

surviving peat house, where peat was dried before being used as fuel, and a large smeltmill. A footpath and bridleway route crosses the watershed past many of these areas, over Greets Hill and Apedale to Castle Bolton in Wensleydale.

Grinton Lodge, a handsome, crenellated, early 19th-century house just above Grinton Gill, is a former shooting lodge and is now a youth hostel with field study facilities.

Just to the west of Grinton along the Harkerside road is Swale Hall, a 17th-century house with mullioned windows. It was here that Daniel Defoe noted the dwelling 'in his abundant vanity of Sir Solomon Swale of Swale Hall in Swaledale, in the County of Swale in the North Riding of York' – Swale had the temerity to suggest, Defoe noted, that the River Swale and its Dale were named after his family and not the other way around. It might have given Defoe grim satisfaction to know that Sir Solomon ended his days in a debtors' prison.

may well have been booty captured by the Brigantes from the Romans and buried for safe keeping. The treasures are now displayed in both the British Museum and the Yorkshire Museum at York.

Moorland roads cross the watershed from Grinton across Harkerside Moor to Redmire and over Cogden Moor to Leyburn. These moors are also riddled with lead-mine workings. Some of the best preserved remains of the lead-mining industry are to be found in Swaledale. Above Grinton on the moors is a

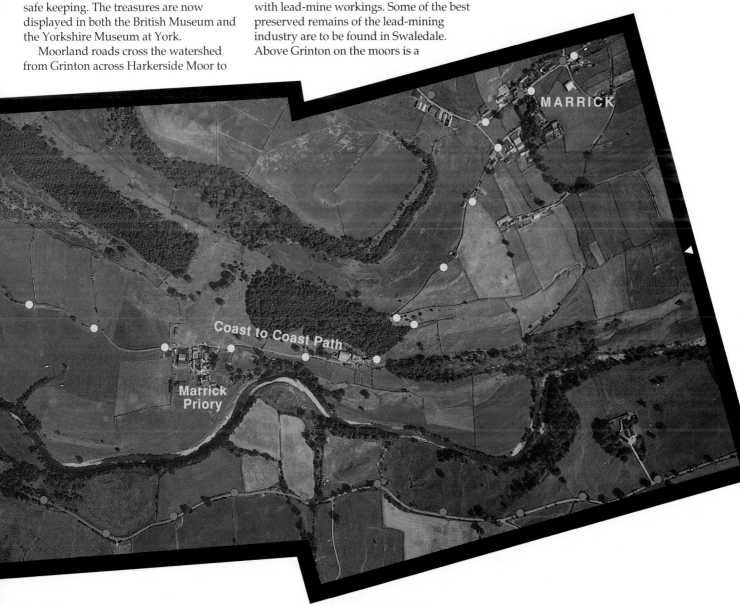

Swaledale

HEALAUGH

River Swale

N

Reeth / Healaugh

REETH IS THE CAPITAL of Upper Swaledale and a natural focal point for the upper dale. It enjoys an elevated yet sheltered position on a high terrace above the River Swale, on the shoulders of Mount Calva. Tall three-storey shops and hotels overlook an extensive village green with a cobbled border and grey-stone pumps, and all is set against a backcloth of rolling pastures and high fells. The green is a glorious sight in spring, when it is filled with daffodils.

Fremington Bridge, on the main road between Fremington and Reeth, is a handsome, neo-classical structure designed by York architect John Carr, better known for his design of Harewood House near Leeds.

Reeth owed its importance and former prosperity to the local lead mines. A charter was granted in 1695 to Philip, Lord Wharton, a prominent Swaledale Quaker, landowner and mining entrepreneur, to hold a weekly market there and four fairs a year. The market has long vanished, but a September agricultural show continues

the tradition of the fairs. But Reeth has declined since the closing of the mines – once its population was over 1,500, but it is now barely a third of that.

The Swaledale Folk Museum, in a cottage just off the green, specialises in material relating to the local lead-mining industry. The London Lead Mining Company, which took over the Whorton holdings in later years, continued the Quaker tradition and in many ways the company was a model employer in terms of looking after its employees. Lead was exported via Stockton not only to London but as far as Hamburg in Germany and St Petersburg in Russia.

Reeth lies at the confluence of Swaledale and Arkengarthdale. Arkengarthdale is a narrow, bleak, almost treeless valley, whose sides are dominated by lead-mining and quarrying activities. Small hamlets such as Arkle Town, Langthwaite (with its delightful village inn), and Whaw lie along the Arkle Beck, linked by a riverside footpath which runs along the sheltered hollow of the valley. Wooded in places, it escapes the exposed bleakness of the surrounding moors.

The main road up the dale ascends the valley side past the CB Inn – named after Charles Bathurst, a local mineowner – beyond Punchard Gill, before crossing empty moorland to Tan Hill, which, at 1,758ft (536m) above sea level, is England's highest and possibly remotest inn. It stands at a crossroads in an area of desolate moorland once celebrated for its coal pits, worked since the 13th century. The inn itself dates from the 18th century and still burns local coal worked from a small seam. Recent boundary changes have returned the inn to Yorkshire from County Durham. A branching road cuts across the valley to ascend Stang Side, crossing The Stang, a 1,677-ft (511m) high pass leading through Stang Forest and Barnard Castle in County Durham, and a spectacular road to negotiate in any weather.

The narrow road which branches southwards from the CB Inn to Healaugh and Feetham bends sharply to cross a shallow ford, a water splash which will be instantly familiar to television viewers from the closing sequence of the Herriot series when it is crossed by the vet's vintage car.

Healaugh is another mining settlement of scattered cottages along a hillside terrace. Many of the cottages were once small farms, combining lead-mining (in the winter months) with the running of a smallholding, which in the summer months helped to eke out a modest living, as well as producing food for a family. Such a pattern was typical of the Northern Pennines. Park Hall, a large farm on the road to the west of Healaugh, stands on the site of a hunting lodge belonging to the Wharton family.

Across the river from Healaugh and cut into the hillside above the Harkerside road is a massive, grass-covered earthwork: Maiden Castle. Some 200ft (60m) across, it is protected by ramparts standing about 15ft (4.5m) above its outer ditch, which were probably even higher and more impressive when first constructed in late Iron Age times. This may have been a second line of defence built behind the Fremington earthworks to defend the Upper Dale against invasion, and suggests the existence of a powerful and well-organised community in the dale at that time.

The well defined earthwork of Maiden Castle can be seen across the river from Healaugh. Footpaths lead up to it from the village.

Feetham / Low Row

THE TWIN VILLAGES of Feetham and
Low Row form an extended community
along the main road up Swaledale.
Feetham takes its name from Old Norse
and Anglian and means 'a settlement by
the meadow', whilst Low Row was the
row of cottages set beneath the higher
track past Blades.

Feetham has a fine old pub known as
the Punchbowl; in former days, fittingly, it
was known as the Miners' Arms. The
Swaledale Corpse Way followed the
bridlepath from Gunnerside on its way
from the head of the dale, crossing over
Low Row Pasture before descending to
Feetham where the pall bearers were
given refreshment before their last stage to
Grinton.

Low Row was the home of the late
Thomas Armstrong, the novelist, perhaps
best known for his novel of Lancashire
cotton mills, *King Cotton*, as well as a fine
and accurately researched novel about life
in the Swaledale lead mines in their
heyday, *Adam Brunskill*.

Religious nonconformity has had a long
life in Swaledale. The first independent
chapel was founded in Low Row by
Phillip, Lord Wharton, in 1691, who was

The ruins of Crackpot Hall. Behind it, spoil heaps from the lead-mines can be seen.

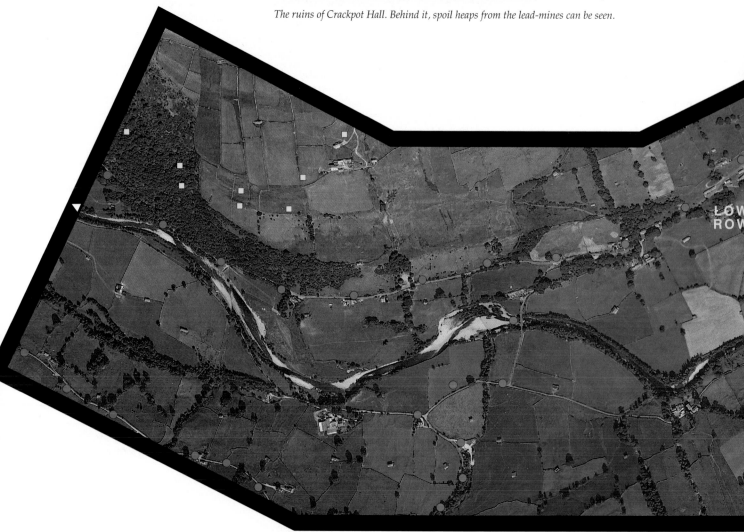

LOW
ROW

also celebrated for his gifts of fine 'Wharton' bibles to local people (see page 103). A property next to Smarber Hall was 'set apart for a public meeting place for Protestants'. The Low Row congregational church, established in 1809, replaced it. It was at Blades, on the hillside above Low Row, that Methodism first came to Swaledale when John Wesley preached there in 1761, as well as in Low Row, and found 'an earnest, simple, loving people'.

In the moors above Feetham and Low Row towards Arkengarthdale there are examples of deep grooves in the hillsides. These were known as 'hushes' and were caused by the simple but effective technique of washing lead ore out of the ground by constructing a large dam in a declivity along a vein on the hillside, behind which a head of water would build up, diverted from a stream. Ore would be loosened by miners with pickaxes and then the dam released, the flood leaving the larger piece of galena (lead ore) behind, whilst the lighter rock and rubble was washed down the hillside. The technique seems to have been

developed from Celtic times and remained in use well into the 18th century, when deep mining techniques came into use. It must have had a devastating effect on the local environment, however, and much of the rubble which was washed down the hillside into the Swale may have helped to cause the river's tendency to flood.

More conventional mining methods have left a massive impact on the moors north of Low Row, an industrial landscape whose relics have a gaunt beauty and are now valued by industrial historians. The streams themselves have names redolent of the activities of 'T'Owd Man', as the miners always called the mines – Hard Gill, Old Gang Beck, Surrender Gill. Old Gang Smelt Mill by Old Gang Beck, with its chimney, is one of the finest surviving lead-mine ruins. However, old mine workings can be extremely dangerous, with deep, often uncharted shafts, and should be avoided except in the company of experienced mine historians and well-equipped potholers.

They are

also often on private land and permission has to be obtained.

The south side of the dale was far less affected by lead-mining, and presents a more rural landscape of scattered barns and isolated farms. These are typical features of Swaledale as are the many small fields. Many of these are particularly rich in wild flowers which make a brilliant display in late spring. Much of Upper Swaledale forms part of the Environmentally Sensitive Areas scheme in the Dales National Park.

Crackpot is a hamlet on the south side of the dale whose name owes nothing to the mental state of its inhabitants, but simply means a cave or pothole where there are lots of crows. The moorland road from Low Whita along Whitaside provides some of the most spectacular views of the dale before climbing steeply across the Fleak Pass into Wensleydale. It is still a good test of a car's gearbox and engine, and is among the first of the northern Dales roads to be blocked by snow in the winter months.

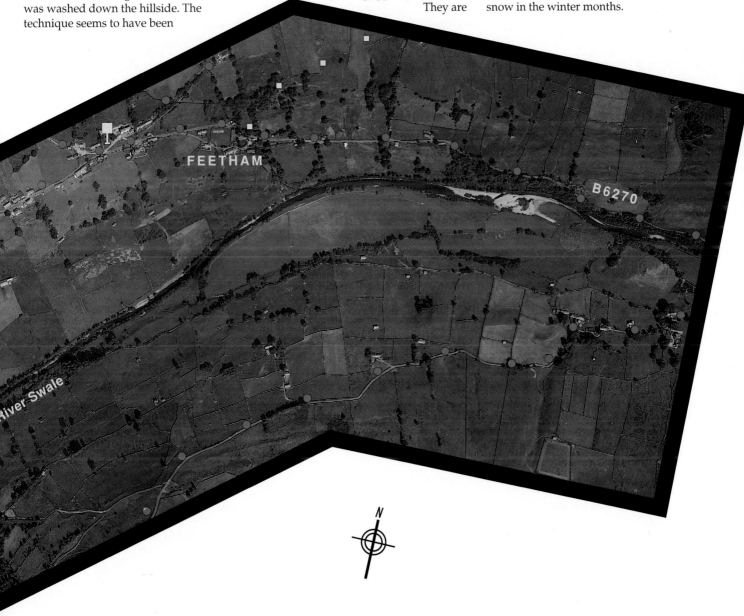

Swaledale

Gunnerside / Ivelet

'GUNNAR' IS STILL a common surname in Denmark, and suggests a Viking origin – the name originally meant 'battle' or 'warrior'. Gunnerside was probably a small farmstead in the Upper Dale, initially only used in the spring and summer months.

The village, like many others in Swaledale, grew rapidly from the 17th century onwards as the lead industry expanded. It was clustered not only alongside the beck where school, chapel, village shop and King's Head inn are still to be found, but along the narrow terraces on the hillside above the main valley and in the tributary valley of Gunnerside Gill. Here you can see many examples of small Dales farms or smallholdings, where subsistence farming and lead-mining in the nearby mines were combined to provide a living for a family. The cottages that form Winter Ings just above Gunnerside Gill are an example: the name indicates the small, more sheltered and south-facing fields in which sheep and perhaps cattle could be overwintered rather than on the higher pastures and fellsides.

Gunnerside Gill is a steep and narrow side valley of the Swale which drains from the high moors on the shoulders of Rogan's Seat and Water Crag. At 2,204ft (671m) above sea level, Rogan's Seat is one of the highest summits in Swaledale, whilst Water Crag to the north, at 2,176ft (663m), is scarcely less impressive. Most of these moors are heather moors, much valued for their grouse shooting, and Land Rover tracks and shooting butts have inevitably made an impact on the landscape.

A network of footpaths (A) leads through the Gill from Gunnerside along the hillside, which is covered with lead-mining relics: old crushing mills, washing floors, spoil tips, and old levels, including Sir Francis Level named after Sir Francis Denys of Draycott Hall, Fremington, landowner and mine proprietor. The marks of old hushes are particularly evident at the top of the Gill around Blakethwaite, where there is a smelt mill and some impressive ruins.

Tracks and moorland paths, including the Coast to Coast path, cross to the Old Gang mines or westwards into Swinnergill, whilst a popular circular walk from Gunnerside goes to the top of the Gill, returning over Black Hill and Jingle Pot Edge and Gunnerside Pasture.

An old track, still a byway used by lead miners, runs along the northern flank of the valley from Gunnerside, leading into Swinnergill. The large house at Ivelet just above the hamlet is Gunnerside Lodge, the home of Lord Peel, descendant of Sir Robert Peel and a prominent local landowner.

The riverside path (B) makes its way westwards through countless small fields, past Ivelet to a former packhorse bridge, spanning the river in a single, elegant stone arch. This bridge formerly carried the main road down the valley, until a new bridge was built at Gunnerside in 1832. Ivelet Bridge also lay on the ancient Corpse Way from Keld (there was reputedly a resting place near the bridge where the corpse could be laid whilst the bearers relaxed) and on packhorse routes from Wensleydale via Oxnop Scar into Swaledale, and perhaps up Stonesdale to Tan Hill and County Durham.

Field paths continue westwards along the riverside past a lovely, broad limestone gorge, lined with trees, where the river tumbles over shallow rapids, or ascend to the hamlet of Calvert Houses

GUNNERSIDE

B6270

River Swale

(literally calf houses) to Muker. This, too, is an area where the meadows are particularly rich in wildflowers – buttercup, cranesbill, campion, margerite, water avens, sorrel – in spring.

Across the river, hidden within woods, lies Oxnop Gill, a steep ravine with a series of small waterfalls formed by Oxnop Beck as it rushes down the Gill. Oxnop Hall close by is a 17th-century farmhouse with narrow, mullioned windows. A datestone indicates the year 1685. A footpath past the Gill offers good views of the falls before it crosses to the road, from where a meandering route can be taken through the fields along the southern flank of the valley, past old farms and orchards into Muker.

The moorland road to Askrigg, climbing from Ivelet past Crow Trees farm and above Oxnop Gill and the long crags of Oxnop Scar, is another test of driving skill. The road ascends and winds across the remote fellside up to Oxnop Beck Head and over Askrigg Common, and on clear days gives superb views in both directions – back into Swaledale or across the wider expanse of Wensleydale to the south.

Gunnerside is built right at the foot of the gill, almost before the bottom of the dale is reached.

Swaledale

Muker / Thwaite

THE VILLAGE OF MUKER enjoys a superb setting to the south-east of Kisdon Hill. A compact village, its little church dates from 1580, when it was built as a chapel-of-ease to Grinton, providing consecrated ground to reduce the need for carrying the dead so far. The route from Keld followed an ancient bridleway (A) across the summit of Kisdon, a magnificent viewpoint along the Upper Dale. The pub where bearers rested – the Queen's Arms – is now a guest house, but the Farmers' Arms exists to supply refreshment to locals and visitors. There is also a photogenic hump-backed bridge, a Literary Institute – the local reading room, a village hall, cafés and shops. Swaledale Woollens is a remarkable local co-operative of farmers' wives, who hand- and machine-knit quality garments, including a range of famous sweaters, from hard-wearing Swaledale wool.

This is the true home of the Swaledale sheep. At the Muker Show, every September, these sturdy, black-faced sheep with their curly horns are exhibited by the Swaledale Sheep Breeders' Association, who use a system of marking pedigree stock by the horns

known as 'crowning'.

Kisdon Hill is a free-standing hill resembling a curious inland island – the result of the River Swale having changed its course due to glacial debris, the original river bed now only containing a small, meandering stream, Thwaite Beck. Hooker Mill Scar, on the south-west face of Kisdon is a glacial scar.

Thwaite is a compact farming hamlet. It was the birthplace of the Kearton brothers, Richard (1862–1928) and Cherry Kearton (1871–1940), who were both pioneer wildlife photographers. The Kearton Guesthouse in Thwaite, a well-known Dales tea shop and restaurant, is named after them, and there is a plaque to their memory outside the old school in Muker.

Thwaite lies at the foot of the Buttertubs Pass to Hawes, one of the most celebrated moorland routes in the Dales, climbing to 1,726ft (525m) over the pass between Great Shunnor Fell and Lady Seat between the two dales. It takes its name from some curious limestone formations by the roadside, deep crevices between tall clints which are fancifully likened to old-fashioned buttertubs. Some of the crevices are up to 100ft (31m) deep. There is now a small parking place and viewpoint area allowing visitors to see the formations in safety.

Thwaite also lies on the Pennine Way which crosses Great Shunnor Fell from

Hardraw, an impressive 2,307-ft (701m) high summit, giving panoramic views, but a bleak and boggy place after wet weather. From Thwaite the Pennine Way crosses the southern shoulder of Kisdon before bearing around the steep eastern side of the summit to Keld, crossing the river at a footbridge below the village just above Catrake Force where East Gill Beck, a tributary stream from Stonesdale Moor, falls in a shimmering cascade over a shallow cliff.

A choice of lower-level paths from both Muker and Thwaite lead to Keld through scattered hazel woods, below steep, craggy hillsides and across lush riverside meadows. A narrow and rocky path gives access down to Kisdon Force, an otherwise hidden waterfall in a deep limestone gorge of the river.

The popular track to the east and north of the river, reached by means of a footbridge north of Muker, offers magnificent views along the Upper Dale and leads to yet more lead-mining remains around Beldi Hill and Crackpot Hall, including Old Field Hush, last worked as a hush in 1846. So rich were the veins that a tramway was built to remove the ore to Beldi Hill dressing floors.

Swinner Gill is a short but impressive side valley, penetrated by a choice of high- and low level paths. Again with extensive lead-mine remains, it includes

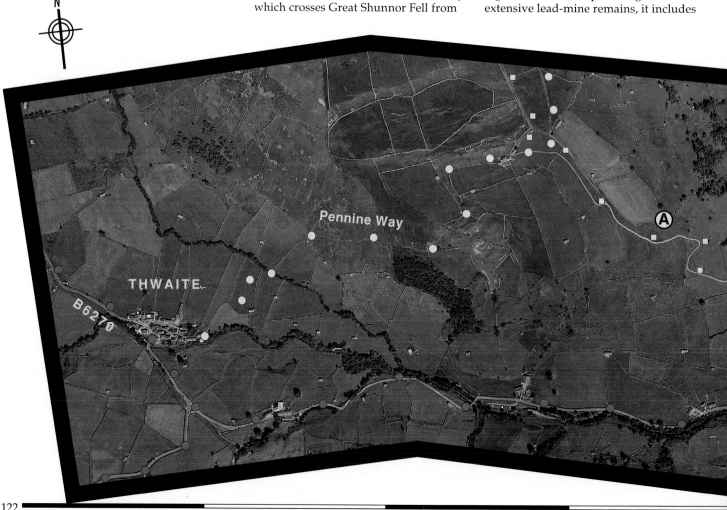

a former smeltmill at the head of the dale. Swinnergill Kirk is the name of a cave which was reputedly used for worship by early Nonconformists in the days of religious persecution.

The B6270, running up the dale from Thwaite, leads around the western slopes of Kisdon, past the hamlet of Angram, (reputedly one of the oldest settlements in the Dales) to Keld, a village that lies around a curious triangle of roads, the main part of the village being at the apex. A youth hostel, limited parking and toilets survive, but the post office and village shop have vanished.

East of Keld the Dale narrows and becomes Birkdale, the river splitting into small tributary becks which have their sources on the surrounding fells. The Swale only takes on its own identity where Great Sleddale and Birkdale Beck meet, west of Wain Wath. Wain Wath Force is another attractive, but this time fairly shallow, waterfall set below wooded limestone cliffs and visible from the adjacent road.

West Stonedale leads northwards, carrying both the road and the Pennine Way up to Tan Hill, whilst Whitsundale extends to Raven Seat. Past Birkdale Tarn the road, now a moorland pass, ascends Birkdale Common to cross Lamp Moss, south of Nine Standards Rigg, into Cumbria and the Eden valley.

Muker, set on the northern side of the road and thus undisturbed by through-traffic, nestles at the foot of Kisdon Hill.

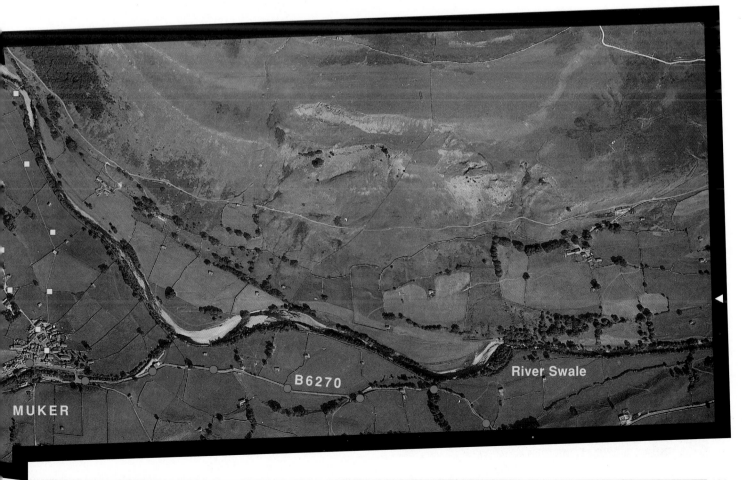

MUKER

B6270

River Swale

Swaledale

Tracks, Roads and Railways

THE PENNINE HILLS have always posed a formidable barrier to the passage of men and their goods. Incredible as it might now seem, in prehistoric times valleys were more difficult to pass through than hills were to cross because of the thick swamp, scrub and impenetratable forest which filled them. It was along the edge of hills or moors, where vegetation was relatively thin, that early hunters and traders could most easily make their way from east to west across the Pennine range.

Many of these moorland or ridgeway tracks have survived. In some cases they have remained in use as tracks, perhaps upgraded into tarmac lanes or moor edge roads. In other cases they no longer carry vehicular traffic, but remain as wonderful 'green lanes' crossing the fellsides. Outstanding examples in the Dales are the High Way which runs between Hawes and Kirkby Stephen around the edge of Cotter End and into Mallerstang, a green road which in the 17th century carried coaches, and which may have been in use as a trade route in Bronze Age times, and the Craven Way, a medieval

Above: The Pennine Way across Pen-y-ghent, probably following an ancient ridge track.

Left: Seventeenth-century Burnsall Bridge now carrying a tarmac road.

Above right: The Roman road near Bainbridge, now a green lane.

Right: The Settle-Carlise railway elevated by Ribblehead Viaduct.

track which goes along the edge of Whernside linking Ribblesdale and Dentdale.

The interweaving patterns of field paths, farm tracks and twisting lanes, which are such an essential feature of the Dales landscape and are so clearly visible on many of the photographs in this book, go back to Anglo-Saxon times, linking individual settlements and homesteads and village centres. Especially important were the Parishioners' Ways which led to the church for worship, or the Priests'

Ways used by the parson to reach outlying chapels in his parish. Many early tracks and roads led to villages such as Grassington or Askrigg where there was a medieval market.

In monastic times, a complex system of trade routes used by trains of packponies carrying wool and other produce was established between outlying farms and granges and the parent abbey. Mastiles Lane between Malham Tarn and Wharfedale was used to transport wool and other produce to the abbey's main

grange at Kilnsey. One route went via Grassington and Stump Cross to Pateley whilst another branch known as Scot Gate went from Conistone over the desolate moorland to Bouthwaite in Nidderdale where there was another grange. Distinctive single-arch bridges, such as those across the Ribble at Stainforth, or across the Swale at Ivelet, allowed packhorse trains to cross often rapidly-rising streams without risk to horse or pack.

In the late 18th and early 19th centuries dramatic improvement of the road system brought good new carriage roads to the Dales and most of them are still the principal main roads of the Dales. One such example is the Lancaster-to-Richmond road which went via Ingleton, Hawes and Leyburn, Hawes growing in importance as a coaching town. Another is the Grassington-to-Pateley Bridge road following the line of the old monastic road to Nidderdale.

Canal transport helped to bring the Industrial Revolution to the edge of the Dales, allowing towns like Skipton to expand with new steam-powered cotton and wool mills. For a time Gargrave became an inland port from where lead and zinc were exported by river and canal to London and Staffordshire.

Railways reached the edge of the Dales in the 1840s with the building of the 'Little' North Western railway between Skipton and Lancaster, which soon had a link from Clapham to Tebay via Ingleton. But the hills created a formidable barrier to railway construction. The Swaledale Line, built to carry Dales-produced lead to the port of Stockton, only went as far as Richmond. Gradually the Wensleydale (Northallerton-Leyburn) railway was extended down the rest of the dale to Hawes. In the meantime Pateley Bridge was linked to the old North Eastern main line at Harrogate, but Upper Wharfedale had to wait until the 20th century to enter the Railway Age when a branch line from Skipton to Grassington was constructed.

The most spectacular railway of all through the Yorkshire Dales is without doubt the Settle-Carlisle line, built between 1869 and 1876 by the Midland Railway to create its own direct main line route to Scotland. It is generally acknowledged to be a masterpiece of Victorian railway engineering, with massive earthworks, viaducts and tunnels. The scale of its architecture reflects the magnificence of the landscape through which it passes. Having narrowly escaped closure in 1989, it is now one of Britain's most popular tourist railways and also a vital local transport link to isolated dales and to Eden valley communities.

Tracks, Roads and Railways

Wensleydale

In recent years, the books and television films of a certain Scottish vet, James Herriot, have given Wensleydale and its sister Swaledale a new worldwide fame. The landscape and characteristic way of life of its communities, not unduly exaggerated by author and producer, now bring North Americans, Europeans and Australians in large numbers.

UNLIKE MOST OF the major dales, Wensleydale doesn't take its name from its river, but from what is now rather a small and relatively insignificant village near Leyburn. For a time the name Yoredale or Uredale was used, after the river, and the little monastery that was eventually established close to the river south of Middleham was named 'Jervaulx' – Norman French for the valley of the Ure. The name Yoredale can still be seen in place names; for example, at Yoredale Bridge, near Bainbridge, and the limestone formations of the higher fells were called the Yoredale series by geologist Professor John Phillips in the 1830s.

The broadest and one of the most typical of the Yorkshire Dales, with extensive, shallow terraces and glacial moraine above its river bed, Wensleydale is a richly fertile landscape. Its farmers have specialised in the production of milk and cheese since the mid-19th century. Milk was taken by overnight express train to the dairies of London and the name Express Dairies still recalls the fast milk trains from Northallerton taking Wensleydale milk to London doorsteps.

Top left: Middleham Castle. The ruins of the childhood home of Richard III are now in the care of English Heritage.

Far left: Aysgarth, with its three waterfalls which cover just under a mile of the River Ure.

Left: Askrigg Common, north of Bainbridge.

Above: Askrigg Pasture, which lies just below Askrigg Common.

Right: Hawes, a busy market town with Gayle Beck flowing through its centre.

Wensleydale

WENSLEYDALE
Aysgarth

AT AYSGARTH, in the centre of Wensleydale, the River Ure tumbles in a series of three major waterfalls and white water rapids – the Upper, Middle and Lower Falls – over gigantic steps carved through the lower beds of hard Yoredale limestone, which are separated by soft shales. Over the years the river has gradually cut back into the rock, creating a deep wooded gorge, now around a mile in length.

Not surprisingly, the falls have long been famous as a tourist attraction. The peat brown waters of the river, breaking to creamy white foam, are especially impressive after heavy rain. A large car park and National Park centre and café cater for the thousands of visitors to the falls, and paths lead up to the Upper and down to the Middle and Lower Falls, the latter through lovely hazel coppiced woodlands – Freeholders Wood. The agile can scramble down to the water's edge at the Lower Falls to enjoy superb views up to the falls from the limestone paving, though care is required when the rock is wet and slippery.

A Tudor single-arched bridge, originally built as a packhorse bridge and only widened in later years, crosses the Upper Falls, providing a fine viewpoint. The tall mill alongside was built in 1784 originally as a cotton mill; it was later used as a woollen and afterwards a flour mill. It reputedly wove the cloth to make shirts for Garibaldi's army, as well as the original balaclavas used in the Crimea, and is now a Carriage Museum with a unique collection of carriages, waggons, horse-drawn coaches, sleds, and even a vintage hearse. Part of the former railway line and path to the falls now forms an attractive nature trail from the car park.

Aysgarth Church stands closer to the village, above the narrow gorge. It was largely rebuilt in the 1860s, but parts of the original 14th-century work remains. Its greatest treasure is a carved wooden screen, dating from around 1506 and brought to Aysgarth from Jervaulx Abbey after the Dissolution.

Attractive walks from the falls car park

River Ure

A684

The Upper Falls at Aysgarth. St Andrew's Church has a lovely 4.5-acre churchyard.

include paths to Aysgarth itself, an unpretentious village with a good cheese shop and a clogmakers. Paths continue up-river (A) through Bear Park to Askrigg, or downriver (B) through delightful beech woods to Redmire Force or, perhaps most satisfying of all, across the fields (C) to Bolton Castle. This magnificent 14th-century castle enjoys one of the most romantically beautiful settings in the north, against a backcloth of fells. Mary Queen of Scots was imprisoned here in 1568 and even attempted to escape – but was quickly recaptured. Her presence was one reason for the abortive 1569 Riding of the North. The castle now contains a fine new museum about its history, and the village known as Castle Bolton is particularly attractive, as is the little, mainly 14th-century, church.

Keen ramblers can take high-level tracks through Bolton Parks and across New Pasture to Ivy Scar. Views along the dale from these higher routes are particularly memorable.

Carperby, easily included on a walk from the falls, or on the return walk from Castle Bolton, is an extended village stretching nearly ½ mile (800m) along the lane. There is a 17th-century market cross on a little green in the centre, the Wheatsheaf Inn (where the 'real' James Herriot went on his honeymoon) and a Friends' Meeting House. The large, long-coated Wensleydale sheep are bred on farms around here, and often used as a cross-breed with other species.

About 8 miles (12.8km) east of Aysgarth, along the A6108 south of Leyburn, is the old town of Middleham, famous for another impressive castle, that of Richard of Gloucester, better known as Richard III. Richard was a highly respected northern leader and in some ways a tragic figure. His castle, with its massive towers, is now owned and managed by English Heritage (open daily), and a weather-worn statue of a boar, Richard's personal symbol, is still to be seen in the top market place opposite the castle. The surviving mound of an ancient Norman motte and bailey castle – known as William's Hill – is to be seen immediately to the south.

West of Aysgarth, the dale opens out to a broader, shallower, less dramatic section of valley. Three roads weave their way along this part of the valley: the main A684 through Aysgarth village, a lane to the south across a higher terrace, past scattered farms and the village of Thornton Rust, and the northern route, which links Redmire, Carperby and Askrigg.

The road to Kettlewell through Bishopdale and across the Kidstones Pass leaves Aysgarth village via Thoralby to join the road from Leyburn near West Burton. This is one of the most perfect of all Dales villages, clustered around its extended village green. Mill Falls, immediately behind the village on Walden Beck, is an attractive if little known waterfall, and paths lead to East Witton over Morpeth Scar, or to the curious ruins of the chapel, once owned by Knights Templar, in a field near Swinithwaite. Stone coffins made for members of the order can still be seen.

At Ballowfield, about 2 miles (3km) west of Carperby, there is a picnic site with access into the adjacent woods. By the riverside immediately to the south is Lady Hill, a rounded hillock capped by a string of pines This glacial drumlin is a notable Wensleydale landmark.

Wensleydale

Woodhall / Askrigg

LOCAL COMMUNITIES WHICH have grown up on each side of the dale between Leyburn and Hawes are still served by separate bus services. This duplication was unnecessary for the former North Eastern railway, which until 1964 ran along the centre of the valley and linked Northallerton with Hawes and Garsdale, with stations at all the larger villages. It now terminates at the quarries at Redmire, from where huge limestone trains depart each day for Tees-side steel works. The track bed (A) is still a feature of the landscape to the north of the river. Some sections (but not all) are in use as a footpath, as waymarks indicate. However, the Wensleydale Railway Association plans to get the line restored for passenger and freight trains. Although the project will cost many millions of pounds, the Association points to the growing traffic problems and pollution suffered by the Dales as car ownership increases, and the need to create good alternative public transport systems.

The hamlet of Woodhall lies down a little lane off the Carperby road and is a scattering of farms and cottages. From here there is access along the old railway or over slightly tricky stepping stones across the river to Thornton Rust – not recommended when the river is in spate.

Nappa Hall, which lies immediately below Nappa Scar on the Askrigg road, is one of the most fascinating houses in the Yorkshire Dales. Dating from around 1459, it is a fortified farmhouse, with a substantial, crenellated tower. For many centuries this was the ancestral home of the Metcalfe family, yeoman farmers and landowners

whose surname is still common throughout the dale. It is now a private house and farm, without public access, but a public footpath passes close by, descending to the bridge over the Ure at Worton.

Because of its importance as a focal point to the dale, Askrigg is really a small town rather than a village, and is rich in history. It was already a relatively large settlement at the time of Domesday, and remained a busy trading centre throughout medieval times. By the 18th century, it was a centre both of hand knitting and clock-making, as well as dyeing, brewing, cotton-spinning and lead-mining. There was a market here between 1587, when its charter was granted, and the early 19th century, when it lapsed. The old market cross still stands in the cobbled market place outside the

churchyard. Fine 18th-century houses, shops and cottages line the main street, and remains of old workshops and workyards still survive to the rear of the frontages.

The church dates from 1175 and has a 15th-century tower, some 15th-century stained glass, a 16th-century clerestory and a Metcalfe chapel.

The choice of the village as the setting for 'Darrowby', and the use of a house in the main street as 'Skeldale House' in the Herriot television films (Herriot's actual surgery was in Thirsk) has made Askrigg a place of pilgrimage for tourists. The King's Head pub has now been subtly de-modernised to look more like 'The Drovers', and an international clientele brushes shoulders with local Dales people at the bar.

A beautiful walk from Askrigg (B) leads to Mill Gill Force, a waterfall in a narrow, wooded gorge whose beck provides a fast flow of water for a surviving mill race. A path to the falls, paved as far as the mill, follows the edge of the steep bluebell woods. The fall itself, a column of water some 70ft (21m) high, fills the gorge with sound and movement. The walk can be extended to Whitfield Gill Force, further upstream. Other walks are up-river to Bainbridge or by a choice of riverside or higher-level routes through to Hawes and Hardraw.

For drivers, spectacular moorland roads cross the fell from Askrigg into Swaledale, to Ivelet and Gunnerside past Oxnop Scar, or across Whitaside to Healaugh and Greets. Both routes offer breathtaking views, but are often among the first roads to be blocked after snow during the winter months.

Wensleydale

Bainbridge

BAINBRIDGE, AS ITS NAME implies, lies alongside the Ure's fast-flowing tributary, the little River Bain. This is reputedly the shortest river in England, being barely 2 miles (3km) long from its source in Semerwater to its confluence with the Ure north of the village.

Bainbridge lies around a spacious and beautifully kept village green, complete with stocks and strategically placed benches. The village is overlooked by Brough Hill, a grassy, flat-topped hillock which was occupied by a small Roman fort, Virosidum, between the 1st and 4th centuries.

The village is celebrated for its remarkable horn, originally blown to guide benighted travellers off the high fells and through the forest; at this time Bainbridge was a meeting place and lodge of the medieval lords of the Forest of Wensleydale. By long tradition, the horn is blown every night at 9 o'clock from 28 September until Shrove Tuesday. A Victorian replica of the ancient horn is kept at the Rose and Crown Inn in

Bainbridge for this purpose. The Rose and Crown itself dates from the 15th century, and was probably in existence during the Forest days. By tradition, the hornblower is a Metcalfe from Wensleydale.

Among many interesting old buildings and cottages around the green and along the banks of the River Bain is a superbly restored water-powered mill, used for grinding corn. All its original machinery is intact and in working order.

The adminstrative offices of the Yorkshire Dales National Park are situated at Yorebridge House by the River Ure.

West of Bainbridge, the river flows between steep, grassy terraces with outlying farms and hamlets occuping the elevated hillsides.

Semer Water, 2 miles (3km) to the south of Bainbridge, is, with Malham Tarn, one of two natural lakes in the Yorkshire Dales. An ancient glacial lake, it is filled by streams from three side valleys – Bardale, Raydale and Cragdale. It covers around 100 acres (40ha), though its size increases after heavy rains. Along

its northern rim is a series of great boulders carried there by glacial action, one of which, the Carlow Stone, is particularly prominent. This boulder features in an often reproduced watercolour of the lake by J M W Turner.

Semer Water is the setting of one of the most famous of all Dales legends. This recalls how an aged beggar, arriving at a village which once existed in the bottom of the valley, was refused food or shelter at every house in the village with the sole exception of a shepherd and his wife in the humblest cottage on a hillside above the main settlement, where the old man spent the night and shared their food. Early next morning the old man – who was an avenging angel in disguise – struck his staff into the hillside and uttered a terrible curse:

Semerwater rise and Semerwater sink
And swallow all the town, save this
   lile house
Where they gave me meat and drink.

Moments afterwards there came a great flood and landslide, engulfing the

entire village and leaving only the cottage, where the shepherd and his wife discovered a heap of gold on the kitchen table when the old man had departed.

This legend may be pre-Christian in origin, recalling the existence of prehistoric 'lake dwellers' or fishermen, traces of whose huts, or pile dwellings, and implements have been discovered along the lakeside. Some years ago a Bronze Age spearhead was found along the shore.

Semer Water itself and the marshy areas alongside the lake are rich in natural history, including rare and unusual wetland plants, making it a nature reserve of national importance, whilst the River Bain is noted for its wild crayfish. The lake is also used for boating and watersports.

Countersett, a hamlet close to the southern edge of the lake, has strong Quaker associations; George Fox stayed there in 1652, and Carr End was the home of the Fothergills, a prominent Wensleydale Quaker family, members of whom helped to found the Society of Friends in America and establish

Ackworth School near Wakefield.

The hamlet of Stalling Busk, to the north, has a melancholy ruined church with tiny cottage windows. When the new church was built in 1908 the old church was simply abandoned to the wind and the weather.

The Roman road across Stake Pass to Bainbridge runs through Stalling Busk.

An equally impressive and remarkably straight Roman road can be traced to the south-west from Bainbridge as it ascends Drumaldrace, heading towards Cam Fell and Ribblesdale. On the summit of Addlebrough, the huge, flat-topped fell, overlooking Bainbridge from the south, traces of Iron Age communities can still be seen.

Semer Water and Malham Tarn in Airedale are the only two natural lakes in the Yorkshire Dales.

BAINBRIDGE

Hawes

HAWES IS THE principal town in Upper Wensleydale, a busy, popular market town on the crossroads between moorland roads and passes from Wensleydale, Garsdale, Ribblesdale, Swaledale and Wharfedale. Its prime position has helped to develop it into an important trading and tourist centre for the northern Dales.

Yet in medieval times Hawes was insignificant in size or strategic importance compared with Bainbridge or Askrigg; it is not even shown on many older maps. In late medieval times the settlement consisted of little more than a chapel-of-ease, established there by Richard III in 1483, and an inn for packhorsemen and their ponies. Its name is derived from 'hause', from old Norse, meaning 'pass'. A market was established here in 1700, suggesting Hawes' growing importance as a meeting point for traders using packhorse routes across the fells.

The building of the 56-mile (89km) Lancaster-Ingleton-Richmond turnpike road in the later 18th century dramatically increased the importance of 'T'Hawes', as it was known. Authorised in 1751, the new purpose-built coach road first used what is now partially the route of the Pennine Way over Dodd Fell and Ten End. In 1791 another road was constructed along the present, more gently graded route through Widdale. Soon mail coaches were rattling their way into Wensleydale, and Hawes became a natural overnight or refreshment stopping point. At the White Hart Inn, in the town centre, you can still see the bell high above the inn door, which was rung by the coachmen to warn passengers that the coach was about to depart. The new road also encouraged the development of small water-powered textile mills in Hawes and its twin village of Gayle.

The other milestone in Hawes' history came a century later in June 1878, when the North Eastern Railway reached the town from Leyburn and Northallerton, to be joined just four months later by the Midland Railway from Garsdale station on the Settle-Carlisle line.

The railway transformed Hawes into a major cattle and sheep market. It also carried farmers and their wives to what has become one of the most popular and busy Tuesday markets in the Dales. It

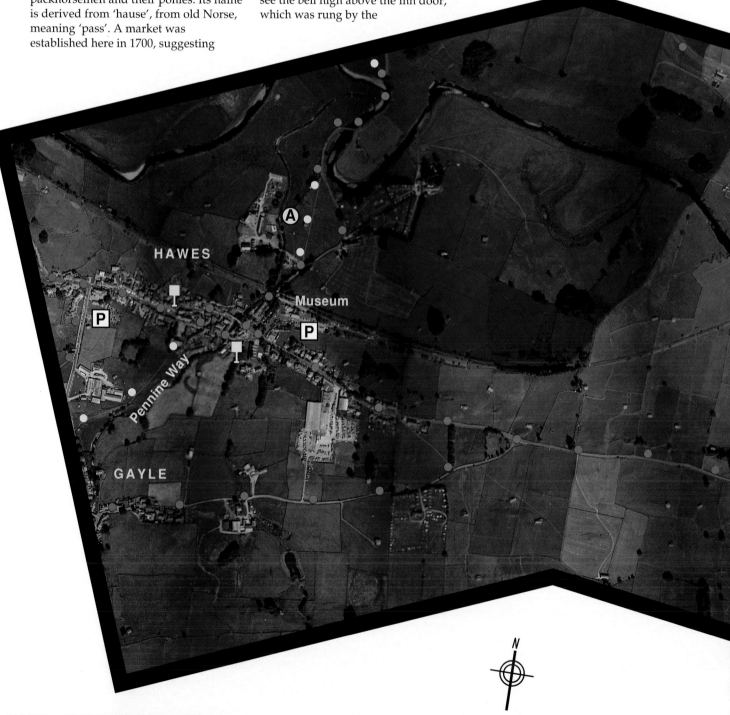

gave a major boost not only to Wensleydale dairy farming but to stone quarrying: vast quantities of Wensleydale flagstones were taken from quarries at Burtersett and Simonstone by cart to be put on freight trains. Stone was transported in particular to the Lancashire cotton towns, where many of the streets are paved with Dales flagstones and houses are built with Wensleydale sandstone.

If Hawes is, in Dales terms, relatively modern, being a mainly late 18th- and 19th-century town, it certainly does not lack interest. It has old shops and pubs, quiet courts and alleyways and several old chapels. The tall Victorian church, with its pinnacled tower, makes a prominent local landmark, visible from fellsides for miles around. Kit Calvert's bookshop, just off the main street, recalls the late T D C 'Kit' Calvert, a celebrated Hawes personality and the former manager of the Wensleydale

Creamery who, during the 1940s, did much to save the manufacture of the famous Wensleydale cheese. This is still made in the modern creamery on the Gayle road. Calvert was a Dales dialect scholar and local historian, and his bookshop – known as the University of the Dales – was the only one in England with an 'honesty box'.

The National Park centre and the Dales Countryside Museum occupy former station buildings in the old Station Yard to the east of the town. The Dales Countryside Museum is based around the priceless collection of Dales agricultural and domestic implements collected by Wensleydale writers and historians Marie Hartley and Joan Ingilby.

A 1½ - mile (2.4 km) walk from Hawes (A), mainly along the flagged fieldpath which carries the Pennine Way, leads to Hardraw where a footpath runs through the centre of the Green Dragon Inn (a small toll is payable as this is a private

path) to one of the most spectacular Dales waterfalls, Hardraw Force. A single, shimmering column of water, 90ft (27m) high, cascades over a lip of hard, Yoredale limestone, pouring over sandstones and soft shales to create an overhang under which visitors can walk without getting wet. The waterfall has, over the millennia, created a wooded gorge which is a natural ampitheatre. This is used from time to time for brass band contests, a Victorian custom which has recently been revived.

With a good choice of accommodation, including a youth hostel, bed and breakfast establishments and small country hotels, Hawes makes an excellent centre from which to explore the northern Dales. Buses operate from Darlington and, at weekends in summer, from Leeds and Wharfedale. A minibus service connects with trains along the Settle-Carlisle line from Garsdale station, but the service must be pre-booked by phone during the winter months.

Wensleydale

The Three Peaks

YORKSHIRE'S THREE PEAKS – Ingleborough, Whernside and Pen-y-ghent – together make up some of the most impressive mountain scenery in the North of England.

This is superb walking country, a landscape of dramatic contrasts with dark, gritstone-capped summits lying above long terraces of limestones. The gigantic steps of the Yoredale Series give the impression of a series of false tops: each steep little ascent yields to another long slope, curving up to yet another craggy limestone or gritstone ridge. The shoulders of all three hills are pierced with deep sink holes and potholes, down which moorland streams plunge. The whole area of the Three Peaks is like a huge honeycomb, riddled with caves and underground passages including the most extended and complex caves systems in the British Isles.

Unfortunately, the area's very popularity has produced some of the worst footpath erosion in the British Isles, where the route crosses areas of vulnerable peat. In some places erosion is so severe that it has scarred the hillsides, and is visible from miles away. Extensive remedial work is currently being undertaken, and signs now direct walkers along restored sections of path in the worst affected areas. Many walkers' organisations are even avoiding the route of Three Peaks Walk altogether, seeking alternative routes in the area.

It is possible to discover plenty of less used routes or more robust sections of path even on the Three Peaks themselves. Other hill tops in the area receive far fewer visitors, and whilst it wouldn't be wise to deflect too many feet to these areas, the discerning hill walker can soon escape to magnificent fell country, away from the lines of coloured anoraks and heavily eroded summit slopes.

Left: The Pecca Falls north of Ingleton.

Above: The ridge of Whernside.

Right: Ingleborough's distinctive summit.

The Three Peaks

Clapham and Ingleton

THE VILLAGE OF CLAPHAM is situated around Clapdale Beck, a fast-flowing stream which comes down from the shoulders of Ingleborough, mainly through the undergound Ingleborough Cave system. Georgian and early Victorian houses and cottages line the village street on either side of the wooded stream. Ingleborough Hall, a neo-classical house in elegant grounds, built in the 1820s, has interior pillars of polished black fossiliferous Dent marble. It is now an Outdoor Education Centre, but for many years was the home of the Farrer family, landowners, scientists and philanthropists, the most famous of whom was Reginald Farrer (1880 – 1920), the world-famous botanist and plant collector. Farrer died in Burma on a plant-collecting expedition in tropical rain forests. Many of his exotic shrub and tree plantings, including superb rhododendrons, exotic conifers and bamboo, brought back from the Far East, and remain in the estate woodland.

A Reginald Farrer Trail through the Ingleborough Estate can be followed from the Estate Office by the woodyard at the

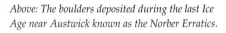

Above: The boulders deposited during the last Ice Age near Austwick known as the Norber Erratics.

Left: Clapham.

Above right: The Pecca Falls on the River Twiss north of Ingleton.

Right: White Scar Caves with Ingleborough in the background.

top of the village. A leaflet is also available at the National Park Centre, situated in the old Manor House by the main car park. The trail follows the carriage drive up into Clapdale Woods (small entrance fee payable), past the artificial lake formed by the damming of Clapdale Beck as it flows through Clapdale from Ingleborough Cave. A turbine above the waterfall, at the lower end of the lake, still provides hydro-electric power for estate workshops. Viewpoints look down into the wooded gorge, and the track passes a small grotto en route to Ingleborough Cave.

Ingleborough Cave is a large, well-lit show cave, first opened up to visitors by the Farrers in 1837, and providing an excellent introduction to the underground world of the Dales with some impressive stalagmite and stalactite formations, flow stone and deep, reflecting pools. It is linked, via flooded passages only penetrable by cave divers,

breadth of the valley. Narrow enclosed tracks lead across to Moughton and Horton in Ribblesdale, and the head of the valley ends in a great ampitheatre of limestone crags, through which a footpath crosses over a natural gap known as Beggar's Stile on to the shoulders of Ingleborough.

At Norber Scar, close to Austwick, is one of the geological wonders of the Dales – the Norber Erratics. These are great boulders of Silurian gritstone or greywacke, which were transported from the head of Crummackdale by glaciers in the last Ice Age, and deposited on limestone pavement, creating pedestals protected from weathering by the boulders. A public path gives access to Napp Scar and Norber from Clapham or Austwick.

Ingleton, to the west, is a popular tourist centre. Trains no longer cross the vast railway viaduct which crosses below this former market and mining town. The site of the former station contains the Community Centre, Tourist Information Centre and main car park.

Shops and cottages line the village's winding main street. The church has a 15th-century tower and a remarkable 12th-century font, carved with scenes from the life of the Virgin Mary. It is a convenient starting point for walks, both to the summit of Ingleborough and around the Ingleton waterfalls, a 4-mile (6km) circular walk along the Twiss and Doe valleys where, in late Victorian times, special walkways were built, with handrails and steps, to allow visitors to enjoy the remarkable series of cataracts and falls which race down the Ingleton Glens. This is one of the most fascinating areas in the Dales for geological exposures, where the fast-flowing streams have carved their way deep into the bedrock. There are pre-Cambrian rock exposures, as well as Ordovician and Silurian slates and Carboniferous limestones. The falls, damp and sheltered, are a good habitat for a wide variety of botanic life – mosses and lichens, orchids and ferns. At Thornton Force, situated on a remarkable geological nonconformity, it is possible to stand on a rocky ledge behind the shimmering curtain of water. Care must be taken at all times to keep children under control by the waterfalls, especially when the rocks are wet, as there are powerful currents and steep banks.

White Scar Caves, close by on the Hawes road, are the largest of the Dales show caves. Discovered in 1923, they are noted not only for their stalactite features, but for their underground waterfalls, and for a natural passageway with a slate floor and limestone roof.

with the Gaping Gill system.

The footpath continues up Trow Gill, a deep, dry limestone gorge fringed with pine trees. Above the Gill, paths can be followed across the fellside to Gaping Gill and Ingleborough summit.

Austwick, reached from Clapham by fieldpath, is a quiet, linear village with a popular inn, the Game Cock. Behind the village lies Crummackdale, a vast, cul-de-sac dale whose little stream, Austwick Beck, seems totally out of scale with the

Ingleborough

INGLEBOROUGH CAN CLAIM to be the cause of the Yorkshire Dales' discovery as a tourist region. In 1761, in the *Gentleman's Magazine,* an anonymous correspondent signing himself 'Pastor' wrote of this 'singularly eminent' mountain with its curious crags, spring and potholes, so flat on its summit that horse races were held there. The article created a great deal of interest, and within a few years poets, painters and topographers were travelling in great numbers to Yorkshire to discover the wonders of what was then known as the Cave District.

Until the late 18th century Ingleborough was assumed to be the highest mountain in England, dominating as it does the surrounding countryside, and visible from both the Lake District and the Lancashire coast. In fact, it is not as high as many Lakeland peaks, and doesn't even match Cross Fell in the North Pennines. Indeed, this is only the second highest of the Three Peaks, but nevertheless gives the impression of being far higher than its relatively modest 2,373ft (721m) above sea level. With Simon Fell and Park Fell, it forms a great complex of isolated fells contained within the triangle formed by Ribblesdale, the Doe and the Wenning valleys.

Historically, the mountain has Celtic associations. The name 'Ingle' is probably of Pictish or Celtic origin, meaning fire, and indicating that the hill top was the site for a beacon. It is also the site of a remarkable Brigantian hillfort, probably dating from the 1st century, and built as a defensive fortification against the Roman legions. The outlines of hut circles and the remains of a wall around the summit plateau can still be traced. One of the most popular routes to the summit, now carrying the Three Peaks Walk, goes up Sulber Nick, a shallow hollow in the limestone, which may have been a Celtic foot and packhorse route to the summit fort. The ruins of a 19th-century summit lodge have been rebuilt as a low wind shelter – a much appreciated facility, given the almost perpetual gales which

Left: Limestone beneath Ingleborough.

Above: Cloud-covered Ingleborough.

Below and right: The very popular pothole known as Gaping Gill.

The Three Peaks

Ingleborough: dramatic snowscapes, Ribblehead Viaduct in the foreground and paths leading to the flat-topped summit.

roar across the summit even when the valleys are relatively calm. Views include the Wenning valley and Forest of Bowland fells, the other two Peaks, the whole of Ribblesdale and the Lancashire coast.

Other routes to the summit are from the Hill Inn, at Chapel-le-Dale along the ridge from Simon Fell and Ribblehead, the relatively little-known fell path northwards from Newby Cote, and the popular routes from Ingleton via Crina Bottom Farm and from Clapham via Trow Gill and Gaping Gill.

Gaping Gill is an immense pothole on the shoulder plateau of Ingleborough, well over 300ft (100m) deep. The shaft leads into the main chamber – a vast cavern some 460ft (140m) long and 98ft (30m) high – the largest cave in Britain. The waterfall carrying Fell Beck into Gaping Gill is the highest in England, albeit underground. It emerges in Ingleborough Cave and Clapdale. Over 9 miles (15km) of passageways lead out of Gaping Gill, one of the most complex cave systems in Europe and a perpetual challenge to experienced potholers and cave divers as much of the system is flooded. Cave diving is one of the most dangerous of all outdoor sports, requiring enormous courage and physical risk. However, many national and European records have been made in Gaping Gill. Other entrances, such as Bar Pot, are now used by cavers as the main way into the Gaping Gill system.

On Bank Holiday Mondays in spring and summer a local caving club – The

Craven Pothole Club – provides a winch service and bosun's chair to take intrepid visitors down to the bottom of the main chamber. Lit by natural daylight, this is one of the most thrilling underground caves in Britain. It is jokingly said that it is free to go down on the Gaping Gill chairlift: you only pay to come back up ! You need to arrive early to take a trip as long queues soon form.

Simon Fell, to the north-west, forms part of the great Ingleborough ridge, linked by a vast saddle in the hills. This is a far less frequented summit, rising as it does to Lord's Seat, a 2,079ft (63m) crag overlooking South House Moor. To the north lies Souther Scales Fell, another National Nature Reserve, designated on account of the outstanding limestone pavements and related wildlife habitats. A path follows the edge of the fell summit above the reserve on to Park Fell, before descending to join the public path at Gauber and Colt Park.

The south-western flanks of Ingleborough contain some of the most impressive limestone pavement and scar scenery in the western Dales, especially along Raven Scar and White Scar where terraces of gleaming limestone contrast with the darker, stepped summit ridge of the mountain peak itself. Most of this pavement area, rich in botanic life, form important Sites of Special Scientific Interest.

The Three Peaks

Pen-y-ghent and Fountains Fell

THE GREAT SPHINX-LIKE shape of Pen-y-ghent overlooks Ribblesdale from the east. It is the most distinctively shaped of the Three Peaks: a great rounded crag rising above a ridge.

At 2,273ft (694m) it is the lowest of the three famous summits, but the final steep ascent up the summit ridge along the Pennine Way from the south, twisting its way across crags and boulders, is as close as many people ever come to authentic mountaineering.

If the name Pen-y-ghent name sounds more Welsh than English, this is no accident. The name is Celtic in origin and probably meant 'hill of the border'. It was quite probably the western edge of the Celtic kingdom of Brigantia which, in pre-Roman times, covered most of modern Yorkshire. The peak would therefore form a natural frontier with the less easily defended Ribble valley. There are memorable summit views, in clear weather, along the whole of length Ribblesdale and across into Littondale.

The most popular route to the summit from Horton is undoubtedly along the Pennine Way past Hunt Pot, an extremely steep ascent to the summit and heavily restored to reduce erosion. The route joins the old miners' path, which slopes diagonally up to the summit wall, stile and trig station. Almost invariably, on any day of the year, there will be a crowd of walkers sheltering behind the wall from the prevailing westerly wind. The alternative route, also part of the Three Peaks Walk, is from Brackenbottom Farm, going steeply up alongside the fell wall and across the limestone outcrops of Brackenbottom Scar and on to Gravel Rigg, before joining the Pennine Way on Fawcett Moor and heading to the summit across the boulder field which forms the face of the mountain.

The Pennine Way eastwards from Dalehead, on the Litton road, actually forms the easiest route to the top, given the relatively high starting-point. The track leads past Churn Milk Hole before crossing on a newer, diagonal alignment to the summit.

To the north, the mountain eases across a gentle saddle to the haunch of the sphinx, Plover Hill. If you know where to look, on the outcrops of the highest limestone crags, you can see the beautiful purple saxifrage, a true alpine flower mainly found in Scotland, but here at one of its most southerly extremities in the Pennines. It flowers in spring, but under no account should it be disturbed, as it is a great rarity.

As its name implies, Plover Hill is the haunt of the golden plover, as well as of the curlew. Paths along the ridge lead to the top end of Littondale, linking with paths down to Foxup and Halton Gill. An alternative route avoiding the summit of Pen-y-ghent, follows the bridlepath along Horton Scar Lane, which leads past Hull Pot and around the edge of the mountain, becoming a beautiful green way known as Foxup Road. This crosses over Foxup Moor before descending into Littondale.

Giant's Grave is a Neolithic burial mound on the eastern flank of the mountain, at the top Pen-y-ghent Gill. The burial chambers lie under a 50-ft

(15m) wide earth mound. Limestone clints have been used to create simple chamber walls: the tumulus probably dates from late Neolithic times, around 2,000 BC.

Fountains Fell is a bleak, inhospitable mountain, known to the thousands of Pennine Way walkers who make their slow way up the winding, peaty path from Tenants Gill over the flat summit. A single, shallow, peaty pool, Fountains Fell Tarns, can be found at the top. However, this summit is also riddled with old shallow coal pits, mainly bell pits. These are a relic of the days when thin seams of often surprisingly good quality coal were found in the Yoredale Series between the shales and the limestones. The seams were worked and used not only for domestic coal in nearby village homes but to burn lime in the many scattered small parish lime kilns. The lime was then scattered on local fields to sweeten the pastures. The old miners' path down the fell above Rainscar Farm, used by generations of miners and their ponies travelling with their loads to and from Stainforth and Horton, now carries walkers along the Pennine Way.

Pen-y-ghent, seen from the west side (left), from Fountains Fell (below) and with the Pennine Way going across the top (right).

The Three Peaks

Whernside and Gragareth

ALTHOUGH WHERNSIDE lacks the dramatic appeal of its two celebrated sisters, it is in many respects equally rewarding to explore. It is a essentially a long, narrow ridge, stretching across the western Dales from Dentdale in the north to Twistleton Scars above Ingleton in the south. At 2,415ft (736m) above sea level, this is the highest of the Three Peaks and the highest summit in the Yorkshire Dales. Its name is a curious combination of Norse and Old English: 'side' is derived from 'saetr' meaning spring pasture; 'whern' (as in 'whin') means millstone, the hard, coarse gritstones of its summit having been used for this purpose. The name can cause confusion with Great Whernside in Wharfedale – 'Great' Whernside in fact being the smaller of the two hills.

It is best to avoid the highly eroded, stony and slippery Three Peaks route directly up the breast of the fell, a great scar in the hillside, and to tackle the mountain from the Dentdale side, leaving the Craven Way, the old green road which crosses from Deepdale to Littledale, at a mid point along the summit of Great Wold. The path leads alongside a wall, eventually passing tall cairns at the end of the summit ridge and the three shallow Whernside Tarns, before following the path to the summit trig station. An alternative route from Ribblehead is to follow the restored path alongside the viaduct and railway, crossing the railway by the aqueduct bridge, beyond the signal box and close to the entrance to Blea Moor Tunnel. The path climbs the side of the mountain past Force Gill, a tiny waterfall in a hidden gorge, to reach the summit ridge.

Views from the summit in clear weather are splendid. Ribblehead Viaduct and station seem like a child's toys below, whilst in clear weather the Lakeland peaks and the Cumbrian coast are clearly visible, as are The Howgills, Wildboar Fell and Ingleborough, itself directly to the south.

A recommended descent back to Ribblehead is via Ivescar and Winterscales; even better is to follow the ridge-top path due south-west over Head Pike and West Fell to join the bridleway along Scale Moor to Twistelton Scars and Ingleton.

Below the southern flanks of the mountain lies a string of small farms with Norse names – Winterscales, Gunner Fleet, Ivescar, Bruntscar, Eller Beck. Close by are several fascinating caves and potholes. Gatekirk Cave is a shallow cave by the stream: Weathercote and Hurtle

Pot were once popular tourist caves, but access is now severely restricted on the grounds of public safety.

To the east of Whernside lies Kingsdale, a narrow valley through which runs Kingsdale Beck and the narrow moorland road between Thornton in Lonsdale and Dent. This crosses the flanks of Whernside before passing old sandstone quarries and twisting steeply down into Dentdale through the fertile beauty of Deepdale. Kingsdale is flanked on either side by impressive limestone scars at Keld Head and Braida Garth.

Kingsdale and Deepdale separate Whernside from Gragareth, a curious mountain shaped like a gigantic question mark. The hook of the question is the northerly peak of Great Coum, the mountain's highest point at 2250ft (686m) above sea level; the stem is the long, narrow ridge above Ease Gill over the saddle to Green Hill, rising to the

three tall cairns on the central summit, called The Three Men of Gragareth. The dot of the question lies in the undulating crags around Tow Scar to the south. There is magnificent, and usually solitary high-level walking along the whole of this great ridge, passing the County Stone where Cumbria, Lancashire and North Yorkshire all meet.

To the south-west Gragareth merges into Leck Fell. This is the only part of the high Dales country which lies in Lancashire, thanks to a long, narrow sliver of the county reaching up to the summit of Gragareth. Ease Gill Beck forms the boundary with Casterton Fell and Cumbria and is a valley of delightful limestone gorges, caves and potholes, including Lancaster Hole, County Pot, Pippikin Pot, Cow Pot, and Bull Pot of the Witches. Several of these potholes give access to extended cave systems reaching deep under the hillsides, and contain

Left: Looking across Whernside to the Howgills.

Above: The summit of Whernside.

Right: The Three Men of Gragareth.

notoriously difficult, quickly flooding sections, where, over the years, many lives have been lost – but where remarkable feats of cave diving and endurance have been executed.

Cowan Bridge, on the A65 just south-west of the village of Leck, enjoys a footnote in literary history. It was the site of the notorious school for clergymens' daughters, known to millions of readers as 'Lowood' in *Jane Eyre,* where, during the 1830s, Charlotte and Emily Brontë and their sisters suffered a harsh regime, finding solace in the beauty of the surrounding countryside. The school is now a private house.

The Yorkshire Dales as a National Park

The term National Park in Britain doesn't mean that the land is nationally owned, nor is it a 'park' in the usual sense of the word. It is an area of specially protected heritage landscape, managed by the National Park Authority which is largely funded by central government.

National Parks have two related primary purposes - to preserve and enhance the natural beauty of the region and to facilitate their enjoyment by the public. However, the National Park Authority must also have due regard to the needs of agriculture, forestry and the social and economic needs of the local community.

The Yorkshire Dales National Park was designated in 1954, and is administered by its own separate management structure, the National Park Authority. The National Park Committee has elected representatives from the two County Councils - North Yorkshire (who administer the National Park) and Cumbria, and from the three District Councils, Craven, Richmondshire and South Lakeland, as well as eight members nominated by the Secretary of State for the Environment. The Park Authority employs a staff of about 80 people who work in two administrative offices, at Bainbridge in Wensleydale and Grassington in Upper Wharfedale. The National Park has its own specialist staff to deal with strategic and local planning matters, including development control, and conservation of both the natural and man-made environment.

Development control means ensuring that all new building harmonises with existing villages and hamlets through the careful use of natural materials and sympathetic design. In the Dales this usually means building in local stone and in traditional local styles. Environmental conservation includes major tree-planting schemes, using native species, and taking measures to protect the distinctive pattern of drystone walls, scattered barns and ancient flower-rich meadows. Much is being achieved in certain parts of the Dales through a scheme administered by the Ministery of Agriculture known as Environmentally Sensitive Areas. This gives farmers direct assistance for the maintenance of walls and barns and encouragement in the form of grants to follow traditional farming methods which aim to protect the herb-rich meadows.

Just as important is the range of visitor services provided by the National Park which include the maintenance of footpaths and bridleways and access areas and the provision of a warden and information services. Wardens, supported by their field service teams, and with the voluntary warden service, have the job of liaising with the local farming community over such tasks as the repair of stiles and footbridges and the waymarking of footpaths. There are also important access areas to look after, including Barden Moor and Fell in Wharfedale, which contain magnificent

Protection and maintenance of stone walls (below left), stiles (right), barns and meadowland (above) is an important part of the Park Authority's work.

Top left: Globe flower – typical of the Dales precious flower meadows.

Below: The provision of well-managed leisure activities is another aspect of the Park Authority's remit.

areas of heather moor and are open to the public thanks to a special agreement between the National Park Authority and the landowners, the Chatsworth Estate.

For most visitors to the Yorkshire Dales, contact with the National Park Authority will be through one of the Park's six strategically placed centres, close by the main car parks at Grassington, Malham, Clapham, Aysgarth Falls and Hawes. These centres have informative exhibitions and displays on various aspects of Dales landscape and history, and a wide range of publications on sale, including maps and guides. They are supported by a network of smaller information points in local shops and post offices.

Among services for visitors provided by the National Park Authority are a guided walks programme led by specialist guides able to interpret various facets of the Dales countryside, and the publication of self-guided walk leaflets and other guides. A free newspaper, *The Visitor*, is produced annually and contains detailed of the Park's activities and walks' programmes. The address for enquiries is the Yorkshire Dales National Park Information Service, Colvend, Hebden Road, Grassington, via Skipton, North Yorkshire BD23 5LB. Tel 0756 752748.

The eastern dales lie outside the National Park, but much of the area, including Colsterdale, Coverdale, Washburndale and Upper Nidderdale, forms part of the proposed Nidderdale Area of Outstanding Natural Beauty which, if implemented, will give this fine area additional landscape protection and positive visitor management.

The Yorkshire Dales as a National Park

The Howgills

THE HOWGILL FELLS are a unique geological and topographical feature. Separated from the Yorkshire Dales and the Lake District by the Rawthey valley to the east and south, and by the Lune gorge to the west, they form a remarkably compact group of hills, a great cluster of long green ridges and smooth, grassy, dome-like hills, rising to over 2,000ft (600m) above sea level in several places.

Geologically, they belong to the Lake District, consisting mainly of a hard, ancient grey Silurian sandstone known as Coniston Grit, probably smoothed over by the action of ancient glaciers. Though locally quarried, and widely used as an excellent building material for houses and farms, you will rarely see Coniston Grit exposed, except around Cautley Crag and Black Force.

Otherwise, the Howgills present a smooth grassy, surface – rough moorland grass or rushes and heather. They are almost entirely treeless. Apart from the occasional sheep fence, they are also largely unenclosed, consisting of ancient common and vast sheep walks to which the public have traditionally enjoyed unfettered access. The Howgills have their own characteristic breed of black-faced sheep, the Rough Fell, whose short legs, long, thick coats and tough constitiution makes them ideally

Left: *A view towards The Calf from Calders.*

Above: *Sedbergh, the main base for exploring the southern Howgills.*

Right: *Cautley Spout and Yarlside.*

equipped to cope with this harsh terrain, and the long, damp winters. There are also herds of fell ponies wandering freely in the area.

Surprisingly, perhaps, the Howgills take their name from an insignificant hamlet on their western flank. These are real mountains: long, wild, open ridges above deep, generally streamless ravines, offering some of the finest views from any hills in the British Isles. But they must also be treated with caution, being dangerous in mist and low cloud with few obvious landmarks for the hill walker. A compass, good equipment and a companion in case of emergencies are essential in all but the most stable weather.

The Howgills

The central and southern fells

Sedbergh, with its good accommodation and refreshment facilities, adequate car parks and even occasional bus service from Kendal or Garsdale on the Settle-Carlisle line, is the obvious centre from which to explore the southern part of the Howgill Fells.

There is good, easy and usually well signed access from the town centre. Although there are few rights of way as such across the fells, well behaved walkers can usually walk freely over the unenclosed parts of the Howgills, though farmers are concerned that walkers should keep to official rights of way across enclosed fields and pastures which skirt the open fell country. Thoughtlessly parked cars can block access tracks or gateways, which can hinder farm access, and dogs need to be kept under control at all times, and preferably left at home during the lambing season (March-May).

From the centre of Sedbergh, a line of three almost conical fells dominates the skyline – Knott, Crook and Winder.

Winder, a mere 1,551ft (473m) high but impressive enough for all that, is Sedbergh's 'town hill', and features in Sedbergh School's Song: 'It's Cautley, Calf and Winder that makes the Sedbergh man'. It has also been a traditional destination, voluntary or compulsory, for a short, lung-bursting cross-country run for generations of schoolboys. If there is only time to climb one of the Howgill summits, Winder must be first choice. It's a steep ascent but not difficult, and within the range of most reasonably fit people.

Access to the summit from Sedbergh can be gained from the fell gate alongside Settlebeck Gill, immediately past Castlehaw, and conveniently signed 'To the Fell'. This route goes part way up along the Gill before bearing off with the path through the bracken on to the little summit ridge. Alternatively, take Howgill Lane, which leads off Main Street by the Golden Lion, before turning right along the track past Lockbank Farm. From here, paths follow the enclosure wall before bearing diagonally right, past the bracken and on to the smooth turf towards the summit trig station. The views across the town and the great basin of the five valleys which feed into Sedbergh are superlative, as are the views northwards into the higher Howgill Fells.

Crook, not quite as high and perhaps a little less spectacular, is nevertheless an extremely satisfying walk from Sedbergh. It too can be reached from the Settlebeck fell gate path; this time the route bears right along an old pipe track and up Ashbeck Gill, a shallow wooded valley

before striking off to the left to curve round to the summit and its cairn.

Knott, at 1,400ft (426m), is the lowest of the famous trio, being more of an outlier. It has been described as the 'cornerstone' of the Howgills and can also be reached along the Settlebeck path, either by following the intake wall before heading direct to the summit, or from the top of Ashbeck Gill, taking in the higher Sickers Fell en route. Views from Knott – the name simply means 'hill' – into Garsdale and along the Rawthey valley are especially good.

Perhaps the finest and most celebrated walk into the Howgills from Sedbergh is to the summit of The Calf, also mentioned in the school song. At 2,220ft (676m), this is the highest point in the Howgill range. The return walk to Sedbergh is about 8 miles (13km), but involves some steady climbing. Again, the fell path from Castleshaw Lane is the obvious starting point, this time going all the way to the top of Settlebeck Gill, the little stream which supplies Sedbergh with much of its water supply, and climbing up to join the old landrover track. This runs over and along the shoulder of Arant Haw and a thrilling, high ridge across a saddle between the fells to Calders. It then

Above and top right: Fell Head, looking north-west and south-west respectively towards the M6.

Right: Black Force with Fell Head beyond.

continues over Bram Fell Top to the summit of The Calf itself, a breath-taking viewpoint. If the weather is clear the Lakeland peaks and other summits in the Dales, including Ingleborough and Wild Boar Fell, will be visible. You are quite likely to see kestrels, ravens and perhaps even an occasional buzzard hovering over the deep gullies that lie between the great rounded domes of the peaks.

You can return by the same route, perhaps taking in the summit of Winder by keeping your height on the ridge from Arant Haw. Alternatively, to make a grand circular walk back to Sedbergh via the Lune valley, head westwards over White Fell Head via Castley and Four Lane Ends, or south-west via Bram Rigg Gill to Birkhaw; or best of all (but not to be tackled in poor visibility), eastwards to Cautley Crag, where a path can be followed down Cautley Spout waterfall, returning via the Rawthey.

These circular routes make for a

splendid, if fairly strenuous, long day's walk back into Sedbergh, covering around 13–14 miles (20–22km); highly recommended, but not to be undertaken in poor weather. In the Howgills the fell walker must steer mainly by the shape of the land and the contours, and there are too many sheep tracks which lead nowhere to make navigation feasible when visibility is poor.

Lonsdale and the western Howgills

The Upper Lune valley – Lonsdale – skirts the western edge of the Howgills south of the Lune Gorge. It is one of the quietest and least known part of the Yorkshire Dales. It was to this part of the Dales that George Fox made his way in June 1652. After preaching outside Sedbergh Church and staying with Richard Robinson at Brigflatts (who later gave land to build the first Meeting House in the area), Fox made his way with a large group of Seekers to a point close to the summit of Firbank Fell and, standing on a rock outside a little chapel, preached a great sermon to over a thousand people, who were so inspired by his words that they founded the worldwide movement known as the Society of Friends, or Quakers.

The rock, known as Fox's Pulpit, can be reached along the back lane which runs to the west of the Lune towards Lambrigg Head, along the top of Firbank Fell. A plaque marks the exact spot where the 'thousand' gathered: access is by a gate from the roadside. From the fell summit there is a magnficent view down into Upper Lonsdale and across to the western slopes of the Howgill Fells. The chapel was destroyed in a gale in 1839, and only the little graveyard remains, but it was rebuilt in the valley below, close to the minor road (B6257) at Firbank.

The river, lane and old railway trackbed share the valley floor. The railway was the ill-fated Ingleton-Tebay line, closed in the early 1960s. A handsome cast-iron viaduct over the Lune near Low Branthwaite is a melancholy relic of this once important line which, had it survived, would have been a valued transport link.

The valley is also traversed by one of the loveliest sections of the Dales Way long-distance footpath as it circles northwards along the banks of the peat-brown, fast-flowing Lune from Sedbergh via High Oaks farm and Lincoln's Inn Bridge. Its route traces paths that link old farms such as Low Branthwaite, Nether Bainbridge and Hole House, before following the riverside through a tree-lined gorge to the Crook of Lune Bridge,

a narrow, hump-backed stone bridge which, until 1974, marked the boundary between the old West Riding of Yorkshire and Westmorland. The Dales Way now veers westwards away from the Dales, heading across the railway and M6 motorway towards Grayrigg Foot and Burneside. A fine brick viaduct, long disused but an impressive monument, carried the old Ingleton railway over the Lune towards its junction with the now electrified West Coast Main line at Lowgill.

The narrow lane which runs along the western flank of the Howgills was originally a Roman road, one of Julius Agricola's campaigning roads which ran from Ribchester in the Ribble valley to Carlisle, following the Lune valley from Kirkby Lonsdale via Middleton. It crosses the Rawthey at a ford, which still exists as a river crossing, west of Sedbergh, and maintained its height above the narrow valley to Low Borrowbridge in the Lune Gorge, where there was a small fort with four gateways.

This lane crosses a steep ravine at Chapel Beck, and links the scattered settlements which make up Howgill itself. It also provides useful access points for walkers to several footpath routes leading to summits along the western side of the Howgills – from Crossbeck to Arant Haw, from Birkhaw to Calders, Arant Haw and

Winder, from Four Lane Ends to The Calf and from Fairmile Gate up to Fell Head – another superb viewpoint.

An especially fine walk is from Low Carlingill (there is usually space to park a car by the roadside) along the Carling Gill valley to Black Force, a deep ravine and small waterfall. A second waterfall, The Spout, is close by. An ascent of Uldale Head can be made from the head of the Gill.

At Fairmile Gate there is an ancient milestone, which may be Roman in origin. Beyond Fairmile Gate, where the old Roman road crosses open fellside below Fell Head, the M6 motorway, A685 trunk road and electrified West Coast Euston-Glasgow railway suddenly emerge from the south-west. They share the narrow and crowded Lune Gorge, heading for Shap and creating what, in transport terms, is a critical road and rail artery between England and Scotland.

This is perhaps the best known part of the Howgills, seen from carriage, car or coach window for a few fleeting seconds by hundreds of thousands of travellers as they speed between England and Scotland, south of Tebay. The great panorama of clustered peaks – Tebay Fell, Blease Fell, Uldale Head and Fell Head – presents one of the most impressive landscape features on the entire journey between England and Scotland.

Unfortunately, the noise from both motorway and railway now take away much of the peace of the landscape. Even though both motorway and railway are dwarfed by the grandeur of the scenery, the incessant traffic drowns the subtle sound of curlew or the rush of wind over the fellside. Only when the walker is well away from direct exposure to the traffic does the roar subside and a sense of remoteness seem possible again.

The northern Howgills

The remote northern Howgills are perhaps the least known and least discovered part of the Dales. They were excluded, for bureaucratic reaons, from the Yorkshire Dales National Park, whose boundary bisects the central ridges of the Howgills. The decision makes no sense either in terms of landscape or conservation, and with luck may one day be reconsidered.

This is countryside of grandeur and austere beauty, richly rewarding and only really accessible to the serious walker – though horse-riders can use the solitary bridlepath that crosses the high fells.

The northern boundary of the Howgills is defined by the busy A685, between Kirkby Stephen and Tebay. As public transport along this road is virtually non-existent, it is necessary to plan circular walks, using a choice of quiet settlements or small laybys off the main road for parking. The nature of the terrain is also perfect for high-level point-to-point rambles across the central Howgills massif.

Ravenstonedale, on the north-eastern corner, is a fellside village whose stone-built cottages lie around Scandal Beck, the stream that flows north to form Smardale before joining the River Eden. It has a particularly interesting church, St Oswald's, built in 1738 and one of the few Georgian churches to be found in Cumbria. Inside, box pews face one another, and a three-decker pulpit has a sounding board and a seat for the parson's wife. The window in the east end of the church commemorates Elizabeth Gaunt, the last Protestant woman in England to be put to death for her faith. She was sentenced to death at the stake in 1638 by the notorious Judge Jeffrey, merely because she sheltered a fugitive, James Burton, who had been involved in the Rye House plot. An earlier church on this site had a separate bell-tower resting on pillars; in its centre hung a refuge bell. Anyone guilty of a crime, no matter how heinous, who managed to escape his or her pursuers to Ravenstondale and who could ring the bell was freed from arrest by the King's officals. The custom, sadly for villains, was abolished by King James I.

Tebay, at the opposite corner of the Howgills, is another ancient village with a fine church, lying on the Roman road, but one whose identity has been drastically altered over the last century and a half, first of all by the railway line, and then by the M6 motorway.

For many years, Tebay was an important railway junction, with lines arriving not only from Lancaster and Carlisle on the main line which opened in 1846, but also from Darlington and Ingleton. It was here that a fleet of banking locomotives was kept to assist expresses and heavy freight to climb the notorious Shap Bank. A virtually new town was built to house all the railway workers required to service the engines.

With the closing of the branch lines and the end of steam, even Tebay station itself was closed, and the vast engine sheds were demolished. In the 1960s the M6 motorway, with its spiral interchanges to the A685 (Junction 38), was constructed

Fell Head, looking north (left), north-east (right) and east (below) towards The Calf.

The Howgills

over part of the prehistoric earthwork by the Lune, and Tebay became a very different kind of town.

Tracks lead direct from Tebay up Tebay Gill, from where there is a magnificent ridgeway on to Knott, Hare Shaw and Blease Fell; it is possible to return via Powson Knott. From Langdale, paths lead further west into deep, secluded valleys such as Langdale and Uldale, climbing to the summit of Simon's Seat, 1,925ft (587m) above sea level.

Bowderdale is another broad, open valley, reached by bridlepath from Bowderdale Foot just off the A685 west of Newbiggin-on-Lune. As the track penetrates deep into the Howgills, it gradually narrows, squeezing between Hazelgill Knott and Yarlside before the final ascent to the summit plateau and The Calf. This is the track that continues over to Winder and Sedbergh, one of the few rights of way in the Howgills.

Another little-known fell walk in the northern Howgills can be followed from Weasdale, west of Ravenstonedale and famous for its hardy tree nursery, claimed to be the highest in the country. This 6-mile (9.6km) circular route takes in the summit of two hills, Randygill Top and Green Bell. Green Bell is the source of the River Lune which flows north towards Newbiggin before turning west to Tebay and the Lune Gorge

On a fellside north of The Calf, on Bush Howe, is the crude outline of a horse known as The Black Horse of Busha, cut into the slaty scree. Opinion differs as to its age and origin, some claiming that it is 18th-century, others believing it to be prehistoric and even maintaining that it has a magic force and is almost impossible to photograph.

The eastern Howgills and Cautley

The A683, which skirts the eastern side of the Howgill Fells between Kirkby Stephen and Sedbergh, is one of the most dramatically beautiful main roads in the Dales, never finer than in late winter and early spring, when snow covers the summits of the fells. Coming from the north, the road switchbacks over open areas of common, past limestone outcrops, to the west of Wild Boar Fell. It continues via Stennerskeugh and Stennerskeugh Clouds before curving past Rawthey Bridge into a narrow gorge, squeezed between the summits of Wandale and Bluecaster.

Rawthey Bridge was rebuilt in 1584 and 1822 to make it safe for stage coach traffic. There are two ancient carved

heads on each side which may well be medieval in origin.

There is an extremely good walk to the summit of Wandale Hill from Handley's Bridge (roadside parking near by). Handley's Bridge is a lovely old stone bridge just to the west of Rawthey Bridge on the A683. The walk can be extended past Adamthwaite, a beautiful, secluded side valley reached by bridlepath above the wooded Wandale Beck, and on to Harter Fell, a broad, open summit.

Murthwaite, on an adjacent low ridge, again reached by bridlepath from Handley's Bridge, is a deserted settlement. The bridleway crosses the shoulder of Hartle Fell to join farm roads northwards to Artlegarth and Ravenstonedale.

Below Handley's Bridge the road follows the River Rawthey, only crossing it at Dowbiggin Foot, with the gentle slopes of Baugh Fell rising up on the left and the massive escarpments of the Howgills on the right. This dramatic difference in landscape illustrates the line of the Pennine Fault as it crosses this section of the Dales, separating their ancient Silurian rocks from the softer Carboniferous limestones, shales and sandstones to the south and east.

At Cautley is a white-walled, 18th-century inn, the Cross Keys, a temperance hotel now owned by the National Trust.

Above and top right: Two views of Baugh Fell from Yarlside.

Right: Bowderdale Beck, which flows northwards into the River Lune.

From the car park layby, a level footpath leads along the valley bottom to two of the most impressive natural features of the Howgills: Cautley Crags and Cautley Spout.

Cautley Crags are a huge crescent of immense, dark crags, several hundred feet high, and the result of an unusual form of glacial action in the Dales. During the last 'little' Ice Age some 11,000 years ago, a small corrie glacier which grew up on the cold north-eastern facing slopes of the mountain, carved and scoured out a deep hollow or bowl beneath the crags, creating the present formidable barrier. Down here a narrow beck, Cautley Spout, tumbles a full 600ft (180m), although it is not a single drop, this is nevertheless one of the highest waterfalls in the British Isles, and a spectacular sight.

A path leads to the bottom of the falls, and the spray creates a microclimate in which ferns and mosses flourish. This is also an area for kestrels and larger falcons, such as sparrowhawks.

The waterfall can be viewed easily

from the path, and the energetic can climb up the side of the falls along another path – more of a scramble – which runs parallel with the waterfall and then round the edge of Cautley Crag on to Great Force Rigg and The Calf. This is a route to be avoided in poor weather conditions, when rocks can be extremely slippery; it is also easy to stray off The Calf on to the sheer cliff face of Crags.

For anyone undertaking a circular walk to Cautley and The Calf, an attractive footpath down the Rawthey valley follows an old bridleway, linking old farms and barns – Cautley Thwaite, Crook Holme, Fawcett Bank and Thurgill. The route follows the banks of the river and is overlooked by the Howgills, under Knott and Crook; it then joins the farm lane back into Sedbergh.

Paths lead from the Rawthey, too, into the western flanks of Baugh Fell, where tracks to the fell peter out in remote gills. The ascent of Baugh Fell is best achieved from this side, perhaps taking in Hebblethwaite Hall, a 16th-century farmhouse where there was once a mill. A path along the evocatively named Ringing Keld Gutter leads to the summit.

Index

Index

Whernside, one of the famous Three Peaks.

Useful Addresses

Countryside Commission, John Dower House, Crescent Place, Cheltenham, Glos GL50 3RA

Forestry Commission, 231 Corstorphine Road, Edinburgh EH12 7AT

National Trust, 36 Queen Anne's Gate, London SW1H 9AS

English Nature, Northminster House, Peterborough, Cambs PE1 1UA

English Heritage, Spur 17, Government Buildings, Hawkenbury, Tunbridge Wells, Kent TN2 5AQ

Long Distance Walkers' Association, 9 Tainters Brook, Hempsted Fields, Uckfield, East Sussex TN22 1UQ

Ramblers' Association, 1/5 Wandsworth Road, London SW8 2LJ

Youth Hostels Association, Trevelyan House, 8 St Stephen's Hill, St Albans, Herts AL1 2DY

The Yorkshire Dales National Park, Colvend, Hebden Road, Grassington, North Yorkshire BD23 5LB

Yorkshire and Humberside Tourist Board, 312 Tadcaster Road, York YO2 2HF

Yorkshire Dales Society, 67 Grove Road, Ilkley, West Yorkshire LS29 9PQ